9-29-59

Values
in the Church Year

Values in the Church Year

For Evangelical Protestantism

William Frederick Dunkle, Jr.

ABINGDON PRESS
New York • Nashville

VALUES IN THE CHURCH YEAR

Library of Congress Catalog Card Number: 59-10359

"Discovering the Calendar" and "Eastertide, the Great Fifty Days" are based on articles that appeared in the January and April, 1958, issues of *The New Christian Advocate.*

SET UP, PRINTED, AND BOUND BY THE PARTHENON PRESS, AT NASHVILLE, TENNESSEE, UNITED STATES OF AMERICA

CAROLYN
always helps

A Preacher's Prayer

O LORD MY GOD,

I am not worthy that thou shouldest come under my roof;

Yet thou hast honored thy servant

With appointing him to stand in thy House.

. . . .

Be ever with me in the performance

Of all the duties of my ministry:

In prayer, to quicken my devotion;

In praises, to heighten my love and gratitude;

And in preaching, to give a readiness of thought and expression

Suitable to the clearness and excellency of thy holy Word.

Grant this for the sake of Jesus Christ . . . .

Amen.

—THE OFFICE OF INSTITUTION OF MINISTERS
The Book of Common Prayer

Introduction

by Bishop G. Bromley Oxnam

THIS BOOK WAS NOT WRITTEN IN AN IVORY TOWER. IT IS NOT an abstract statement of liturgics. William Frederick Dunkle, Jr., is the pastor of a city church. His schedule is crowded. He faces the heavy obligations and privileges of a great parish. He confronts the inexorable demands of an exacting pulpit. He says, "I have discussed the calendar as a journeyman pastor writing to fellow craftsmen who minister to congregations." He does just that.

This book is therefore a handbook, a practical book, a stimulating book.

It is based upon the oath taken by a witness when he is sworn. The witness is pledged to tell not only the truth, but the whole truth, and nothing but the truth. Dr. Dunkle knows that ministers are in danger of riding their intellectual hobbies, of reading their favorite passages, and of thus presenting only a segment of the truth. He believes that a partial presentation of the gospel is inadequate, that the study of "all of the Bible" is essential, and that while "some biblical truths deserve more emphasis than do others," nevertheless the "whole truth" must be preached. When he himself analyzed his own preaching, after a careful study of what the Church Calendar means, he says, "I was shocked to learn how little of the whole Scripture, even how little of the whole New Testament, even how little of the Gospels, I had treated in my preaching." And facing the fact "that many of our people do not read their Bibles at home," he asked, "Dare we continue to leave them in ignorance of the Scriptures?"

Dr. Dunkle insists that as the general educational level of the nation rises, frontier and primitive conditions no longer obtain. It is wrong, he concludes, "to keep evangelical Protestants oriented to frontier folkways."

Values in the Church Year is not an uncritical plea for the Church Calendar. Dr. Dunkle declares, "The gospel itself is not controlled by seasons. Jesus Christ is the same yesterday, and today, and forever. In other words, the Calendar does not make the Christian message; exactly the opposite is the truth. . . . It is the evangelical's business not to preach the church calendar but to preach the gospel of Christ." The evangelical must be on guard lest he preach "Advent sermons, or Christmas sermons, or Epiphany sermons, or Lenten sermons." He must never forget that he is called upon to preach the gospel in Advent, at Christmas, during Epiphany and Lent. But Dr. Dunkle continues, "The Calendar has helped me avoid some of the individualism which plagues the Protestant pulpit." It is made abundantly clear that preaching is guided by the great themes of the Church Year. It is preaching that will traverse the whole realm of biblical truth. It is not preaching shackled by a plan but preaching full of variety and possessing balance.

The use of a lectionary and of the Calendar means that there is a "working relationship between the pulpit and the whole Bible." The Free Churches will not be bound by rigid and mechanical requirements in this matter. It is a matter not of law but of grace. Such a gearing of preaching and of Calendar, Dr. Dunkle believes, ensures broad biblical coverage, prevents inappropriateness, offers ready-made but sound sources for sermonic materials, prevents "the tedium of overemphasis on a few biblical themes," enlarges the range of the preacher's personal study, and enhances the variety, color, and interest element of the homiletical product.

Dr. Dunkle knows that the individual no doubt can work out his own program of preaching which will involve the whole range of biblical thought, but this is not only hard work but unnecessary work, since it has been done in the emphases of the Church Year. He is wise enough to emphasize that lectionaries are not meant to be mechanical; "they serve only as vehicles for grace."

But the book is much more than a plea for the discoveries of "values in the Church Year" for evangelical Protestantism. It is a record of practice in this field by a distinguished and imaginative minister. It will prove to be particularly helpful to others who are ready to experiment. The sermon themes that Dr. Dunkle has discovered as he has traversed the Church Year are set down in captivating fashion. His suggestions are not to be confused with crutches. Rather they are in the nature of summons to walk with eyes front, shoulders back, and at rapid pace.

Dr. Dunkle knows that we have lost much by our failure to follow Easter with the resurrection message. He deals with the mountains that are associated with the life of Jesus, and moves from Mount Calvary "to that last unknown hill in Galilee" with the intriguing sermonic theme of "His Last Mountain." The Ascension, upon which so few ministers ever preach, becomes a mountain experience.

The texts Dr. Dunkle suggests are full of fascination. For instance, for Labor Day he suggests, "Labour not for the meat which perisheth, but for that meat which endureth unto everlasting life." And again, "Whatsoever ye do, do all to the glory of God." And in the light of contemporary problems the text from Gen. 15:11, "Birds of prey came down; . . . Abram drove them away." (R.S.V.)

This is indeed a practical book, a book that may result in the enrichment of preaching, certainly one designed to help ministers bring breadth to preaching, depth to preaching, decision to the preaching hour. It is a book that calls for "the truth, the whole truth, and nothing but the truth," and in outlining the values that lie in the Church Year, points a new way for evangelical Protestantism.

Foreword

THE DIFFERENCE BETWEEN A DENOMINATION AND A SECT IS that the former is concerned about its catholicity while the latter in its self-sufficiency doesn't even care whether or not it is catholic. While treasuring still the special contributions most of us feel our own denominations have to offer, few evangelical Christians today would insist that any denomination is the complete Christian Church. Earlier generations of churchmen were much surer than we are of the rightness and wholeness of their respective communions and of what they felt were the errors of all others. Nevertheless, we do want to be right and whole, do want very much to be members of the Church catholic, the Church Christian, and to be so accepted. We are as zealous to claim our full and rightful place in catholic Christianity as our fathers may have been jealous to defend denominational particularisms as the only true teachings of the New Testament. That means, I take it, that we are becoming more interested in catholic Christianity than in merely primitive Christianity.

But the two are not mutually exclusive, and this is what

Protestant Christians today are learning more and more. Catholic churchmanship, developed and modified by generation after generation, is rooted in primitive practices and has slowly produced the standards by which the changeless truths of the New Testament are best preserved and proclaimed.

The thesis of this book is simply that the most practical point for evangelical churchmen to start practicing catholic Christianity is the Church Calendar.

For the Calendar is thoroughly catholic in the sense that it arranges for the proclamation and observance of the whole biblical message in yearly sequence, as the Church in many ages and many lands and many branches has best learned to ensure that nothing essential to the Christian witness be overlooked. The Calendar has grown and is still growing, and this ensures its essential catholicity. Evangelical Christianity has much to give it and ought to start doing so instead of ignoring it.

Already this is under way. Free Churchmen are learning rapidly in our generation that there may be genuine evangelical content in the Calendar's seasons and sequences. The use of the Calendar is no longer supposed to imply that a minister and his congregation have "gone Gothic" or "high church," or become ritualistic, formal, or sacerdotal. The Calendar is the first point of compatible contact between the evangelical spirit and catholic churchmanship, because it is the easiest and simplest contact to make. American Protestants can use the Calendar without necessarily using any special ceremonies, vestments, or colors and without ascribing to any new doctrines or to any one viewpoint about ministerial orders. The Calendar is something all

Christians can follow together, gaining fellowship with one another in a common catholic practice without losing any special denominational values or without departing from the New Testament faith.

Throughout this book I have tried to keep in mind a Presbyterian, Congregationalist, Baptist, or Methodist reader or one from some other evangelical communion. But before addressing his brethren across denominational lines, I suppose a writer ought to present his ecumenical credentials. I received a B.D. degree from a seminary related to one denomination and a Th.M. degree from a seminary related to another denomination. I have served as an officer of a state council of churches and as president of an active metropolitan council of churches. I have also enjoyed membership on commissions of the former Federal Council of Churches and present National Council of Churches. All this means, I hope, that I can testify out of my most valued ministerial experiences that there is a genuine catholicity in all evangelical Christianity and a common, growing interest in the recovery of vertical or historical continuity as well as in the development of horizontal or inclusive fellowship. As I have lived and labored in several parts of America and felt the finest possible fraternity with fellow Christians of many communions, I have come to know that we are all deeply implanted as branches of the one, holy, and catholic Church.

At this very point I hope you will see the connection which explains why throughout this writing I call it the *Church* Year rather than the Christian Year. It is true indeed that the Calendar is a cycle of seasons centering on Christ, his meaning and message. This is why most churchmen call it the *Christian* Calendar. But I do not think the observance of the Calendar will necessarily help us to be more Christian. I think the Calendar can help churches to be *the Church* and then in turn help us make a better proclamation of and witness to our common Christianity.

Among other things, all this experience has convinced me that unless evangelical churchmen can relate the Calendar closely to preaching, it will never enter the life of American Protestantism. This is the only reason I have offered homiletical material at all in this book, just to illustrate and demonstate the values of the Calendar. For example, a fellow Free Churchman might shy away from observing Advent unless he can appreciate that there is no danger of running out of Advent sermons. His first supposition might be that Advent would tie him too rigidly to a single theme four Sundays out of every year. So I have tried to indicate some of the variety possible in Advent preaching. On the other hand, the respective themes of single days such as Christmas, Easter Sunday, Pentecost Sunday, and Trinity Sunday are already well known to us all; and so I have not felt it necessary to suggest for them extensive sermonic treatments. It really isn't neccessary to seek variety for occasions which occur only once a year. This, then, does not intend to be a book of sermons or even primarily a book about preaching. Rather, if I can forward the appreciation and use of the Calendar itself among my friends, they will preach far better sermons than I can suggest here. The Calendar is a very useful preaching aid, and that is all I wish to demonstrate.

Another conviction which has grown out of the ecumenical fraternity I have enjoyed with fellow evangelicals is that

American Protestants are above all else practical churchmen. They will not care greatly how old a tradition is or how universally observed it may be if it is not useful and meaningful in modern church life. Accordingly, I have discussed the Calendar as a journeyman pastor writing to fellow craftsmen who minister to congregations. Whatever historical content there is in this book is incidental, and you will discover that there are only a few vestigial remains of scholarship left from my university seminary days which haven't quite been squeezed out yet by parish pragmatics. I am writing about the uses and values of the Calendar, not about the Calendar as such. Therefore, this is "shop talk," not by a specialist but by a general practitioner of the parish ministry.

Here is why I think this book needed to be written:

The need all of us have who have been reared in the Free Churches of America is to adapt our ministries in the last half of the twentieth century to a liturgical cultus with which our fathers and grandfathers (mine were parsons) had almost completely lost contact. This is the ecumenical trend of our times. We can rebel and resist. We can be faddish. We can be slavish imitators. Or we can adjust gracefully and intelligently. If we do the latter, we can take with us into a new orientation all the best values of evangelical witness.

All I have tried to do is to show how this can be done. For younger ministers this book may be an introductory orientation, including some warnings against mistakes I myself have made. For men of middle years this is an attempt to relate past background to new developments without jarring evangelical sensitivities and to talk only of the "possibles" or those liturgical uses which won't get us in trouble with our people in churches as they are now.

Here I must thank my colleagues of several denominations and students in various pastors' schools who, both in groups and as individuals, have helped review and revise the subject matter of this book. I have tried to check with as many ministers from as many communions as possible nearly all of what I finally have written, as this work over a period of years has evolved from a master's degree thesis to a series of lectures to some published articles to this book form. Sincerest appreciation is expressed also to Miss Dorothy Litz for her invaluable assistance as my secretary.

I think I know that the need which I have tried to meet is real. Some present-day evangelicals will keep on ignoring the Church Calendar. Time's ordinary calendar will not ignore them, and in due season they will depart from us. Some contemporary evangelicals will appreciate that the Calendar which seems so new is indeed very old and will look backward to recover its values as they move forward in its framework to serve better each present age.

WILLIAM FREDERICK DUNKLE, JR.

Contents

Discovering the Calendar

"Everywhere avail yourself of the great festivals, by preaching on the occasion."—*John Wesley*

I SHALL NEVER FORGET MY PERSONAL DISCOVERY OF THE ancient ecclesiastical Calendar. Like all young preachers in their first pastorates I was running up against the hard reality that Sunday after Sunday, week after week, regardless of every other claim and duty, I was expected to preach. I enjoyed preaching and still do. But there's a vast difference, I soon learned, between the enjoyment of preaching occasionally and the necessity of preaching regularly. Every Sunday night when I went to bed, I found myself wondering what to preach about the following Sunday. It was like my wife's feeling toward washing dishes. As soon as one meal's dishes were washed and dried, it almost seemed time to start all over again with the next meal's dishes. You never felt you were getting ahead of the game.

The problem, of course, was what to preach *about*. If one could have some idea of the general theme, it wasn't too difficult to discover scripture texts, illustrations, and so on. But week after week I struggled through that first year grabbing at ideas here and there for the subject matter of my preaching.

Then one day near the end of that first year I happened to be thumbing through my denominational hymnal. By sheerest chance my eyes fell on that page in one of the indexes which listed the Church Calendar, giving suggested lections for each of the days and seasons. Well, there it all was—First Sunday in Advent, Second Sunday in Advent, Epiphany, Ascension Sunday, and so forth. Here was something new to me. Oh, to be sure, I knew vaguely that there were these ancient days and seasons in Christian tradition. But they had never seemed to have any relationship to the worship life of evangelical Protestants as I had known it. Maybe Christmas and Easter, or Palm Sunday and Good Friday, perhaps, or possibly even Pentecost Sunday, but here for the first time I began to see the whole planned circuit of the seasons.

It looked good to a boy preacher. It seemed to present the possibility of a plan, and I badly needed a plan.

For several years I have studied and worked to know the uses of the Church Year, its origins and meanings, its implications and sequences. It still looks good to me, and this book represents my desire to share this experience with my fellow ministers of like background in evangelical Protestantism. It's my way of saying, "Here's a good thing we can use, and here's why I think so."

How long man has been sensing something sacred in the recurring seasons, nobody knows. Certainly it is a very ancient thing and may be seen in all the earliest religions. The Israelites had their Sabbath and their religious calendar, and the earliest Christians had their Lord's Day and began even in the first centuries to develop an ecclesiastical Calendar.

The historical development of the calendar has been briefly summarized in *The Christian Year*, edited for the Federal Council of Churches in 1940 by Fred Winslow Adams:

> It was at first an outgrowth of some features of the Jewish ritual year, but was recentered by the growing experiences of the primitive church. The general observance of Easter by 150 A.D. was followed by Lent, Ascension Day, Pentecost, Christmas, and Epiphany, all of which were in vogue by the fourth century. The Advent season probably had its rise in Gaul and was given its permanent place by Gregory the Great in the sixth century. Trinity Sunday was not added until the twelfth century. In the seventeenth century the Reformers overhauled the Roman and Sarum missals, making considerable modification and adopting new and elaborate lectionaries which have continued to our day. . . .
>
> If the proper and united observance of Sunday, the Lord's Day, is a value never to be surrendered, why longer neglect a united observance of the Lord's Year? . . . .
>
> The Christian Year is a compass whose needle always points to Christ. From the beginning it has been a means by which the whole Church could be aided in realizing His divine Presence. When Jesus said at the Last Supper, "This do in remembrance of me," he had sown the seed of the Christian Year. Following His resurrection, the Eucharist began to be celebrated every Sunday or First Day of the week. Eventually, the Jewish Sabbath was transformed into the Lord's Day, the Jewish Passover into Easter—the Festival of the Resurrection, and the Jewish Pentecost into Whitsunday—the Festival of the

outpouring of the Holy Spirit. It was natural that Jesus' birth should also be observed. Thus a Christian Year was born. It was organized about a desire to remember Christ by worshipping in His Name and surrounding the Name with Festivals commemorating events of His life. The entire Calendar was thus arranged as a litany of adoration. The Christian Year circles around the Light of the World. Its seven seasons all tell of Him.

Strictly from the preacher's viewpoint, however, the values of the Calendar may be listed thus:

1. *Here is a plan.* From week to week through year after year the preacher may look ahead to what is coming. The use of the Calendar for planning his preaching enables a preacher to accumulate homiletic materials with some foreseeable use in mind. To illustrate, he can know in June that when next January comes he will be observing the Epiphany season with its emphasis on Christian missions, and the good missionary stories and ideas he gleans from his reading in June can be filed for specific use in sermons he may already have in mind for January. He can look ahead to find the best places for "spot sermons" required by denominational programs. To continue the illustration, he can plan to preach the annual race relations sermon on a Sunday in Epiphany when it will have natural connection with the preaching already planned for that period.

2. *Here is balance.* Preachers, like most people, are tempted to ride their hobbies. Christian missions is a highly important theme, but a minister actively engaged as a member of his denominational missions board, for example, may find himself preaching about Christian missions most of the time to the neglect of other equally important

aspects of the total Christian message. Centered on Christ as it is, the ancient Calendar leads from one major Christian consideration to another from season to season throughout every year. A preaching program adjusted to it will be a balanced one in which all of the paramount claims of the gospel and every basic doctrine of Christianity will have been presented in some form in the course of each year.

3. *Here is variety.* American evangelical Protestantism suffers from dullness in many of its practices. It tends to lack movement, color, drama, interest. While the Calendar *seems* to be a fixed and prescribed pattern, actually it is an arrangement of changing emphases. In his book *Planning a Year's Pulpit Work*, Andrew W. Blackwood formerly of Princeton Seminary, commented on the Christian Year: "Even in the bodies that prescribe readings and prayers for public worship, the clergyman is largely free to determine what he shall preach."

Within each major season there is an almost infinite variety of homiletical treatment possible. The Calendar suggests the singing of far more hymns, the reading of passages from the *whole* Bible, the preaching of sermons on *all* instead of merely some basic Christian doctrines. And all this, in turn, suggests a variety not now apparent in many, if not most, of our evangelical churches.

My preacher father once said to me, "Son, what many ministers seem most to lack is a *sense of occasion.*" By that he meant a feeling for the fitting, an appreciation of the appropriate. This will be illustrated in reverse when I tell you that I once knew an iconoclastic brother whose sermon title for Easter Sunday was "Camping on the Highroad to Hell." Now granting for the sake of argument that this sermon needed to be preached, I submit that the good brother demonstrated an almost total lack of any sense about time and place. He had no sense of occasion. I am confident that he offended deeply the people who came to church that Easter Sunday expecting a message on the resurrection theme, and that he failed utterly to gain an effective hearing for a sermon on any other theme.

The ancient Calendar of Christendom is calculated to develop in ministers of the gospel, as well as in Christians generally, an understanding of the gospel in its entirety as applied specifically from year to year to the recurring seasons and to the great devotional occasions. Almost unconsciously in all of us there are feelings peculiar to summer, autumn, winter, and spring, to Christmas, Easter, Lent, and Advent, which provide the emotional and psychological setting in which the gospel must be preached. My conviction is that Protestant preachers need to be far more sensitive than they generally are to the necessity of adapting their homiletics to this factor. The Calendar is a tested adaptation.

It will require a sensitive sense of occasion, for example, to handle two observances on the same day, but that situation often occurs. One year, I remember, Mother's Day and Pentecost Sunday fell on the same date. The average evangelical Protestant congregation in America expects a special observance of Mother's Day and a sermon appropriate to that occasion, though gradually we are gaining a transference from Mother's Day to the Festival of the Christian Home. On the other hand, Pentecost Sunday has a message too vital to be ignored. The solution, it seemed to me, was to preach a Pentecost sermon about motherhood. From the story of Pentecost I found this text, "And on my handmaidens I will pour out in those days of my Spirit . . ." (Acts 2:18) I think my sermon from that text did no violence to the expectations of the people on Mother's Day, but in addition it enabled me to preach about the Pentecost experience of the Holy Spirit. Now when Pentecost Sunday and Aldersgate Sunday fall on the same day, as in some years they do, the preaching situation will be almost ideal. Who could fail to sense the relationship between the Pentecost of the Upper Room in Jerusalem and the pentecost in the little room on Aldersgate Street in London when John Wesley felt his heart strangely warmed? Increasingly Aldersgate Sunday is being observed by other denominations than Methodism, interestingly enough by Episcopalians most of all.

Sometimes current events will have their effect on a preacher's sense of occasion. As Harry Emerson Fosdick said to his homiletics class at Union Seminary, our preaching must "snuggle down closely against life around us," and we must have so heightened a sense of occasion that we can adapt the great themes of the gospel to the observances both of the Church and of the human society in which the Church lives.

For that matter, the Church itself often demands a considerable skill in arranging our preaching in order to match denominational observances to the Calendar. If your fiscal church year requires that the annual every-member canvass begin the first Sunday in October, for example, there is no need to ignore World Communion Sunday that same day. Rather, use the two occasions to mutual advantage. Help your people to see the Church of Christ as a great world-wide fellowship and therein all the more reason to pledge their financial support to the Church as an institution.

Or when annual periods of evangelistic emphasis are expected, enhance their value by relating them to appropriate seasonal settings. Lent with its natural emphasis on personal religion is an excellent time for revival services. The late spring and early summer during Whitsuntide form natural occasions for preaching missions, emphasizing the work of the Holy Spirit in human hearts. Even Kingdomtide in the autumn may be related very meaningfully to the need for enlarging church membership, winning new citizens for Christ's kingdom, or spreading the Church's influence in society.

Fortunately, many of our denominational agencies and interdenominational councils are beginning to develop a sense of occasion. The united women's organizations have instituted the World Day of Prayer for the first Friday in Lent, and boards of missions have seen the values in having the annual missions study classes in every congregation during the Epiphany month of January, to cite but two examples.

As means to an end Christians of all denominations have learned that the days and seasons of the Church Year are valuable utensils in the work of the Kingdom. Increasingly we are using them, and we must learn to use them more and more effectively. They are the mountaintops from which we shout God's glory, the valleys through which we walk humbly with our God. From year to year as the seasons come and go, we preach a saving gospel in all its parts, perfect and whole. Over and over again, yet with infinite variety, we proclaim the unsearchable riches of Christ, the old, old story ever new and wonderful. Along the well-charted paths of the Calendar we are learning to walk the way of faith, finding that it is marked with fixed and tested milestones which keep us from getting lost or straying off. Yes, when we have sensed the seasons and hallowed all our time, we can say with the Psalmist that truly "day unto day uttereth speech, and night unto night sheweth knowledge."

HOW THE CALENDAR GOES

Advent begins with the Sunday nearest to November 30, so occasionally the first Sunday in Advent will be in November, but usually all of Advent is in December. Advent is always four Sundays, so the Sunday before Christmas Day is *not* Christmas Sunday, but the fourth Sunday in Advent.

Christmastide begins with a vigil on Christmas Eve, December 24, and always contains the Sunday after December 25. Sometimes there is a second Sunday in Christmastide as this season does not end until after New Year's or, in some countries, until Epiphany.

Epiphany is always January 6, and the number of Sundays in Epiphanytide may be from four to nine, depending on the date of Easter Sunday.

The three Sundays before Ash Wednesday (called Septuagesima, Sexagesima, and Quinquagesima respectively) are sometimes observed not as Epiphanytide but as Pre-Lent.

Lent begins on Ash Wednesday, which is forty-six days before Easter Sunday. Passion Sunday is two Sundays before Easter Sunday, and Palm Sunday is the Sunday before

Easter Sunday. Palm Sunday introduces Holy Week in which are Maundy Thursday and Good Friday.

Eastertide, the Great Fifty Days, begins on Easter Sunday, climaxes on Ascension Day (Holy Thursday) forty days later, and culminates on Pentecost Sunday (or Whitsunday) fifty days later.

Trinity Sunday is the Sunday after Pentecost Sunday, and the Sundays following it may be numbered either after Pentecost Sunday and called Whitsuntide or after Trinity Sunday and called Trinitytide.

Kingdomtide begins the last Sunday in August and continues until Advent begins. If Kingdomtide is not observed, Whitsuntide or Trinitytide are continued through the autumn until Advent. All Saints' Day is November 1.

Note that the date of Easter Sunday controls the position and length of several days and seasons. Easter Sunday is the next Sunday after the first full moon after the vernal equinox, but what that really means is that every minister must buy a calendar every year to find when Easter Sunday is coming, or ask the minister in the next nearest church, or find out from somebody. The so-called World Calendar, which has been much proposed but little adopted, would solve this problem by fixing Easter Sunday invariably on April 8. From now through this century Easter Sunday under the present variable arrangement will fall on the Sundays indicated here:

1959	March 29	1980	April 6
1960	April 17	1981	April 19
1961	April 2	1982	April 11
1962	April 22	1983	April 3
1963	April 14	1984	April 22

1964	March 29	1985	April 7
1965	April 18	1986	March 30
1966	April 10	1987	April 19
1967	March 26	1988	April 3
1968	April 14	1989	March 26
1969	April 6	1990	April 15
1970	March 29	1991	March 31
1971	April 11	1992	April 19
1972	April 2	1993	April 11
1973	April 22	1994	April 3
1974	April 14	1995	April 16
1975	March 30	1996	April 7
1976	April 18	1997	March 30
1977	April 10	1998	April 12
1978	March 26	1999	April 4
1979	April 15	2000	April 23

Advent, Christmas, and Epiphany

THESE THREE CLOSELY RELATED SEASONS, ALL ONE GENERAL period, begin the Church Year. Christmas is one of the two greatest festivals which commemorate Christ, the other being, of course, Easter.[1] The great doctrine of the Incarnation is lifted up during this period, as is the Resurrection during Eastertide.

Each of the great festivals is preceded by a season of solemn preparation. For the festival of Christmas the penitential period is the Advent season, just as for Easter the preparation is Lent. The Advent season always embraces the four Sundays preceding Christmas Day. The value of this season is largely lost, however, if Christmas celebrations, musical services, pageants, and so on are employed too soon before Christmas Day itself, though in the face of secular commercialization it is difficult if not impossible to keep the distinction between Advent and Christmas clear in the minds of the average evangelical congregation. The dominant theme of Advent is Christ's coming—both

[1] Unfortunately Ascension Day has never had this primary rank in evangelical Protestant observance.

his first coming to earth in the Incarnation and his ultimate establishment of the kingdom of God on earth—and our Christian responsibility to be ready to receive him worthily.

Christmas is not a day but a *season* of eight days, called an "octave." Traditionally it begins with the vigil of Christmas Eve and continues for eight days thereafter. Strictly speaking, Christmas Sunday is always the Sunday after Christmas unless Christmas Day itself should fall upon a Sunday. Most evangelical Protestants observe Christmas Sunday on the Sunday before Christmas Day, however. Obviously the central theme of Christmas is "the Word made flesh," the birth of Jesus.

The Feast of the Epiphany is always January 6, which in parts of the Eastern Church is still observed as Christmas. It commemorates the coming of the three Wise Men to Jesus. They were perhaps the first Gentiles to whom he manifested himself, and thus the Epiphany season is the great period for missionary emphasis—Christ's manifestation to all the world, to both Jew and Gentile. The number of Sundays in Epiphany will vary, depending on the date of Easter Sunday for any given year. The more traditional Calendars will introduce three Sundays (called *Septuagesima, Sexagesima,* and *Quinquagesima* Sundays) between the beginning of Lent and the end of the Epiphany Season. Since Lent itself is forty days in duration, not counting Sundays, these pre-Lenten Sundays add even more days to be counted until Easter Sunday, and hence the relative numbering of these three Sundays in relation to Easter Sunday is suggested in their respective Latin names. The Church Year suggested in 1940 by the former Federal Council of Churches of Christ in America, however, included in the Epiphany season all Sundays between January 6 and the beginning of Lent proper.

Within this whole period will fall certain other occasions, not all of which are universally observed. The second Sunday in December (which sometimes will be the third Sunday in Advent) is called Universal Bible Sunday when the American Bible Society stresses the importance of the Scriptures. New Year's Day in the civil year is, of course, January 1, and some evangelical Protestant groups observe Watchnight on New Year's Eve. Liturgical churches usually observe such days as the feasts of St. Paul, St. Stephen, St. John Evangelist, Holy Innocents, the Circumcision of Christ, and so forth, within this period. The Church Year of the Federal Council suggested that January 1 may be observed as the Festival of Christ's Christening.

The interdenominational council on missions has designated the second Sunday in the Epiphany sequence as Missionary Sunday. Race Relations Sunday, the Sunday nearest Lincoln's birthday anniversary, and Brotherhood Sunday, the Sunday nearest Washington's birthday anniversary, both in February, may come within this general period during some years, depending upon the lateness of Easter Sunday in any given year. When the Epiphany sequence suggested by the Federal Council of Churches is followed rather than the traditional Calendar, the likelihood that these two occasions will fall within the Epiphany Season is increased.

This whole period centering around Christ's nativity, then, is rich in preaching possibilities. For Advent one might plan a series of sermons on the doctrine of Christ's coming: his coming to earth in the Incarnation, his Kingdom coming into all the areas of the world's life ever since; his ultimate coming in judgment, righteousness, and equity. In observance of Universal Bible Sunday one may well define the Scriptures as the pattern of his coming Kingdom and as the principal channel by which the truth concerning this coming Kingdom has been made known to men. Throughout Advent emphasis will be given naturally to the necessity for *preparation*, personal and social, to receive the Kingdom and to hasten its appearing. But in addition to certain traditional Advent emphases, this season also may be adapted to a variety of other preaching themes. For example, during one year's Advent season, I felt it entirely appropriate to preach on the Christian ideals of marriage, courtship, parenthood, and so forth. Here is an outline of this Advent series which may illustrate the adaptation:

First Sunday in Advent: Matt. 25:6, 13—"Behold, the bridegroom cometh. . . . Watch, therefore . . . . " The Church as the Bride of Christ prepares itself all the time for his visitations. It *expects* new experiences of his grace and is watchful for them. This is how the Church remains young, vigorous, and growing and how it avoids becoming settled, staid, satisfied. If this is good for the whole Church, it is no less good for individual Christians, particularly young Christians. They are perfectly proper when they are expecting great and new experiences, especially the experiences of true love, marriage, parenthood. They are wise and wholesome when they prepare themselves for these experiences and learn how to be watchful for these experiences and learn how to be watchful for the distinguishing signs between true and false love. The Church may very appropriately create opportunities and environment where the expectations of young people may be fulfilled, and the Church has a great responsibility in providing guidance for young people who are watching for the mates God may give them.

Second Sunday in Advent: Luke 1:35—"The Holy Ghost shall come upon thee, and the power of the Highest shall overshadow thee: therefore also that holy thing which shall be born of thee shall be called the Son of God." Mary, Joseph, and the blessed Babe we call "The Holy Family" and remember as such especially near Christmas. This helps us renew the household holiness of our own families, realizing afresh how very holy indeed is the partnership we may have with God as parents. Nothing we may do shares more of God's creation than the bringing of new lives into being. The privilege of procreation is indeed "the power of the Highest" loaned to us, so the sweetness of sex must never be cheapened by what the world calls "sexiness." Every child born or borne of our bodies truly "shall be called the son of God," and this demands the most intelligent preparation on our part for every child's coming: a preparation of ourselves spiritually to be good parents, a preparation of our social order to offer good opportunities to our children. When we become parents, the Holy Spirit comes upon us and may be received within us.

Third Sunday in Advent (Universal Bible Sunday): Deut. 29:29—"The secret things belong unto the Lord our God: but those things which are revealed belong unto us and to our children for ever, that we may do all the words of this law." In previous generations the so-called "Family Bible" preserved on its flyleaves a record of births, marriages, deaths, and so forth. But the Bible's own words are still the best record of God's dealing with his children. It is still the best way we preserve and pass on those basic ideals on which successful families are established and maintained. Nobody knows all the secrets of God, but what he *has* told us through his word and law is completely sufficient to make us the family of God, as were our parents and as may be our children.

Fourth Sunday in Advent (next before Christmas Day): Luke 2:12—"And this shall be a sign unto you; ye shall find the babe . . . ." If we have learned to call Mary, Joseph, and the infant Jesus "The Holy Family," we should remember that it was the Babe who made this a holy family. Wherever we find a baby, we see a sign or reminder of responsibility and chiefly of the responsibility to be holy. Things we might permit ourselves to do, we dare not indulge for our children's sake. Children save us from selfishness. Children make us hope for holiness.

Christmas Sunday (Student Recognition Sunday in several denominations): Luke 4:16—"And he came to Nazareth, where he had been brought up . . . ." Jesus had been away from home—to the River Jordan to hear the prophetic wisdom of John the Baptist, out in the wilderness to learn the lessons of truth revealed to him there. As our students are home for the holidays, sharing with us the family festival of Christmas, back from their learning and lessons, so Jesus had come home to Nazareth. He shared what he had perceived and apprehended away from home with those who had remained in the family congregation of his home-town synagogue, and this we must gladly receive from our own sons and daughters. He announced his vocation as an encouragement to his friends and family. We hope our own young people will do this. He resumed the spiritual customs of his heritage, as we invite and urge our own young men and women to do. If he was not honored in his own family community, we must be sure that this will not be felt by the students who are here today.

Sometimes it may be not only entirely appropriate but also effective to carry a connection of title or theme through the whole nativity period, embracing Advent, Christmastide, and even Epiphany. I tried to do this once with titles this way:

ROADS TO BETHLEHEM

The Highway of Holiness	Isa. 25:8
The Highway of Hope	Luke 2:15
The Highway of Haste	Luke 1:39
The Highway of the Humble	Luke 2:4
The Highway of the Heart	Luke 2:19
The Way of the Wise	Matt. 2:1

An examination of the texts will suggest the content of these sermons, there being no great originality in my treatment, but the titles at least illustrate how the series carried over into the beginning of the Epiphany season.

Advent is so clearly connected with Christmas, despite the important distinction between the purposes of the two seasons, that almost always a sermon series begun in Advent will continue through Christmastide if not into Epiphanytide. This can be done not only with titles but also with a single text. For example, I found in Wilbur Fisk Tillett's beautiful hymn repeated lines which suggested the general title "O Word of God Incarnate" which in turn suggested naturally enough the great introductory lines of the Fourth Gospel and was worked out in an Advent-Christmastide series this way:

A WORD OF GOD INCARNATE
John 1:1, 14 (R.S.V.)

An Original Word—"In the beginning was the Word."
A Divine Word—"And the Word was God."
A Human Word—"And the Word became flesh."
A Living Word—"And the Word . . . dwelt among us."
A Saving Word—"And the Word became . . . full of grace and truth."
A Glorious Word—"We have beheld his glory, glory as of the only Son from the Father."

The cover page of an Advent bulletin will illustrate how a single text can be used throughout a season, in this case with the title coming from a supporting text. (See page 38.)

Still another way of developing continuity through two seasons without losing the values of either might be a group of sermons related to one another in their general title and mutual affinity such as "Songs of a Young Faith," a general title for the earliest hymns of Christianity: the Magnificat (Luke 1:46-55), the Benedictus (Luke 1:68-79), the Nunc Dimittis (Luke 2:29-32), and the Angelic Chorus (Luke 2:14). For Christmas Sunday itself, always the Sunday after Christmas Day, might be added "Songs Our Faith Sings Now" based on any of the carols in modern use.

Of course, there is no requirement that a *series* of sermons be preached at any season. Certainly no series should be enterprised just to be homiletically clever if the real message and meaning of a season is ignored. It does seem true, however, that Advent particularly and the nativity period generally lend themselves well to the series

> **The**
> **Advent Season**
> **1957**
>
> **"A Name Above Every Name"**
>
> ***Sermons of the Season***
>
> *Isaiah ix:6* "For unto us a child is born, unto us a son is given: and the government shall be upon his shoulder: and his name shall be called
>
> **December 1:** . . . Wonderful,
> **December 8:** . . . Counsellor,
> **December 15:** . . . the Mighty God,
> **December 22:** . . . the Everlasting Father,
> **December 29:** . . . the Prince of Peace.
>
> *Philippians ii: 9-11* "Wherefore God also hath highly exalted him, and given him a name which is above every name: that at the name of Jesus every knee should bow, of things in heaven, and things in earth, and things under the earth; and that every tongue should confess that Jesus Christ is Lord, to the glory of God the Father."

treatment. The number of Sundays involved is compact, and there is a general public acceptance of the idea that an identifiable season is being observed. Series at any time also have the advantage of attracting special attention, which one hopes is reflected in attendance.

But for Advent itself here are some standard texts:

Mark 1:14-15—"Jesus came . . . preaching the gospel of the kingdom of God, and saying, The time is fulfilled, and the kingdom of God is at hand: repent ye, and believe."

I Cor. 4:5—"Therefore judge nothing before the time, until the Lord come, who both will bring to light the hidden things of darkness, and will make manifest the counsels of the hearts: and then shall every man have praise of God."

Luke 12:45—"If that servant say in his heart, My lord delayeth his coming . . . ."

Luke 12:56—"But how is it that ye do not discern this time?"

Traditionally, of course, these have been regarded as adventist and eschatological scriptures. Moreover, there is no denying that recent generations of liberal church people have all but lost any doctrine of Christ's return or any interest in what earlier Christians called "the last things." Since, however, this strain undeniably runs all through the New Testament, surely preachers of today have a responsibility to find for today's church people meanings that are truly meaningful. If so, what better time to meet this challenge than in the Advent season?

Christmastide itself is by now too thoroughly established in the life of all churches to need any extended emphasis here. Everybody knows that it is not actually an anniversary of our Lord's birth and that it represents early Christianity's conversion of the winter solstice, a great pagan festival. It is clear that the conversion has not yet been made perfect, for that matter. Christmas may still be regarded as Christianity's extreme front sector in its warfare with the world. That's why Christmas still needs the support of the Advent period of serious preparation. Suffice it to say that if one may rise above the sentimentalities and rise against the secularities which surround the yuletide, Christmas is a time for great preaching about Christianity's great theme, God made man to save the world. The season's scriptures are known by heart and still speak to hearts their old, old story. No need to strive for uniqueness, to be original or clever!

A preacher's practical problem, however, is that he must proclaim (sometimes in weakness and weariness he almost thinks the word is "exploit") that central Christmas subject several times within a few days every year. Although it is technically the fourth Sunday in Advent, the Sunday before Christmas Day is expected to be thoroughly "Christmasy" by the average evangelical congregation. Then there will be needed a sermon for Christmas Eve or Christmas Day, one for the real Christmas Sunday after Christmas Day, and undoubtedly one or more for various Christmas occasions planned by organizations within a church or its community. Even if he cannot hope to be original, a preacher must at least be ingenious in arranging his Christmastide sermons. It may be some illustration of that to take a few Christmas clichés and try to breath some new life and spirituality into their hackneyed words:

"Shop Early"—Don't wait until life has made you jaded, tired, hurried, and harried to experience the meaning of Christmas or until your response to God's redeeming love is no longer joyous, fresh, vibrant.

"Don't Open Until Christmas"—It is a great, but glorious mystery that God was all along giving himself to the world but waited until the birth of his Son to unwrap the wholeness of his great love, when the fullness of time had come, as if he had said to history, "Don't open until . . . ."

"Gift Wrapped"—In swaddling clothes, in the protection of a manger's straw, in the love of a pondering mother, in the adoration of Judean shepherds, in flesh that veiled the very Godhead came, gift wrapped, the Saviour of the world.

"Dreaming of a White Christmas"—More than snow is needed to cover the tracks where sin has walked, to make pure and fair a world in which the vision of justice and equity has never quite died; and more than dreaming will bring the reality of Christ's blessed kingdom.

At any rate, the basic theme of Christmas needs no arduous discovering, and the uses of that theme have no limit. No minister lives long enough to preach all the Christmas sermons. Even if he did, people would hear them all over again gladly. Nobody gets tired of the Christmas story! (Except maybe a preacher after five sermons within eight days.)

Ah, but the Epiphany season offers the best possible change of pace! After the Christmas holidays is a time to call a congregation to workaday religion. Advent has been called "the season of expectancy" and Epiphanytide "the season of the Evangel." What better time to gird again for the evangelization of the world than as a New Year opens? It's a time for starting over again and yet again on the endless mission.

Race Relations Sunday and Brotherhood Sunday within

Epiphanytide call for gripping and grappling with the hard realities of Christianity's mission. Those Wise Men who traveled from the East brought a breadth to Christianity at the very start which makes the Epiphany season a time for scope and range in defining the meaning of the Christian mission, which makes the Evangel global and social and not solely individualistic or pietistic. There's power and punch in Epiphany preaching. Or there ought to be, for the Epiphany means much more than three little boys dressed up in bathrobes for a Sunday-school pageant.

Something of this magnitude that is in the Epiphany evangel may be found in the Creation doxology, Gen. 1:31 —"And God saw every thing that he had made, and behold, it was very good." At least this doesn't limit God's concern, or comfort those who still put "home missions" over against "foreign missions." Consider the application of this text to race relations. Ring the changes on how much there is which God first saw as good and which we must now confess is wrong in all our world. A companion to this last idea is suggested in another missionary text I have used in Epiphanytide, I Cor. 16:9: "For a great door and effectual is opened unto me, and there are many adversaries."

Light is the ancient symbol of Christ's manifestation. An increasing number of churches dramatize this in pageants and music and occasions coming to be known as "The Festival of Light" during Epiphanytide. Preaching can reflect this also. The star of Bethlehem is a constant suggestion of light. Here are some texts:

Phil. 2:15—"That ye may be blameless and harmless, the sons of God, without rebuke, in the midst of a crooked and perverse nation, among whom ye shine as lights in the world."

Eph. 5:14, the well-known Epiphany introit—"Awake thou that sleepest, and arise from the dead, and Christ shall give thee light."

Ps. 67:1-2—"God be merciful unto us, and bless us; and cause his face to shine upon us; . . . that thy way may be known upon earth, thy saving health among all nations."

John 8:12—"Then spake Jesus . . . , saying, I am the light of the world: he that followeth me . . . shall have the light of life."

Perhaps an observance of the civil New Year and the Epiphany emphasis on missions could be combined with the use of Hab. 3:2—"O Lord, revive thy work in the midst of the years."

Frequently there are denominational programs to be considered in midwinter. Many churches launch their financial campaigns at the start of each calendar year. One year, I remember, there was a denominational emphasis on church-school enrollment in January and February. I arranged the old standard missionary text this way:

"Go . . .	"Go to the People!"
Ye . . .	"Who Else but You?"
Therefore . . .	"Our Heritage of Learning"
And Teach . . .	"Truth Must Be Taught"
All Nations"	"From Here to Everywhere"

Even narrowly defined the subject of missions deserves more than a single sermon a year. In its broadest meaning missions is the only logical response of discipleship to the faith proclaimed in Advent and Christmastide, and therefore, the preacher who neglects the third act in the great drama of the Nativity or who fails to use to the fullest the opportunities of Epiphanytide is surely offering his people a truncated gospel and a crippled Christianity.

Lent, Passiontide, Easter

THE AXIS OF OUR LORD'S LIFE IS FIXED ON TWO POLES—the Incarnation and the Resurrection. Around the first, we have seen, clusters the Nativity season, or Advent, Christmastide, and Epiphany. Now comes Lent, the season of fasting and preparation for the observance of Passiontide and Eastertide, which with Ascensiontide is related to Christ's resurrection.

In America, at least, the three pre-Lenten Sundays following Epiphanytide proper are not generally observed by the evangelical Protestant bodies, especially those which follow the suggestions of *The Christian Year* originally published under the auspices of what was formerly known as the Federal Council of the Churches of Christ in America which continues the "Sundays in Epiphany" right up to the beginning of Lent proper.

These three transitional Sundays between Epiphany and Lent might be used to emphasize one's denominational or confessional formularies about holy living. For example, a Presbyterian might use the Shorter Catechism for sermons on "My Duty to God," "My Duty to Others," "My Duty to

Myself," or a Methodist might preach on Wesley's General Rules, "Do No Harm," "Do All the Good You Can," "Attend upon the Ordinances of the Church." Almost every branch of the Church has some historical document from which such a series of treatments might be derived as an introduction to Lent.

Lent proper, though, actually begins with Ash Wednesday, forty days before Easter Day not counting the Sundays. The Lenten fast was practiced in the ancient Church as early as the year 130, though probably not for the full forty days now observed.

The word "Lent" is probably derived from the Anglo-Saxon *lencten*, or spring, which in turn may have derived from the Anglo-Saxon *lang*, or long, because in the spring the days get longer; so there is no especial significance in the name itself as in the case of most other occasions in the Calendar. It is simply a period coming in the springtime of each year.

Ash Wednesday itself is a comparatively late observance. Roman Catholics and Anglo-Catholics observe it as a day of fasting (commemorative of the biblical phrase "sackcloth and ashes" to connote profound sorrow and penitence), and one of the ceremonies is the marking of each worshiper's forehead with the black ashes or soot left from the burning of the previous year's Palm Sunday palms.

For evangelical Protestants also Ash Wednesday may be a day of penitence and self-examination. Many Protestant churches which commonly have a midweek prayer service on Wednesday nights may make the observance of Ash Wednesday a high point in the year's week-night worship. One very ancient and catholic practice which has peculiarly evangelical associations and which would be highly appropriate for Ash Wednesday night is the New Testament *agape* or love feast. One way to make it dramatic is to ask every worshiper to bring a candle with which to light the church, which is exactly what our frontier forebears did when they announced that a service would be held "at early candlelighting." Another traditional announcement would be that after the hour of worship arrives, the doors will be shut and late-comers not admitted, though this originally meant that only members in good standing were expected to participate in a love feast.

At any rate, it seems a shame that Protestants haven't developed their own observances for Ash Wednesday, calculated to heighten the significance of the beginning of Lent, as the observance of Lent has become well-nigh universal in these latter years. Ozora S. Davis, in *Preaching on Church and Community Occasions*,[1] wrote in 1928 that "the annual season of Lent is now observed to an increasing extent among the nonliturgical churches; and it is reasonable to anticipate a still further extension of the practice."

Passiontide is a subdivision of Lent—a term usually applied to the last two weeks including Holy Week. During Passiontide, if that term is used, Lent is still in progress, so either term is perfectly admissible. However, Lent does approach its climax during its closing days, and the death, or passion, of our Lord does draw nearer to the consciousness of Christians during the week before and the week of Good Friday, so Passiontide as a designation does express some meanings. The fifth Sunday in Lent is commonly called Passion Sunday, so named because in the Anglican

[1] The University of Chicago Press.

lexionary the gospel for that day refers to Christ's Passion. The sixth Sunday in Lent is almost universally observed as Palm Sunday in commemoration of Christ's triumphal entry into Jerusalem. Between Palm Sunday and Easter Day lies the so-called Holy Week, which also is observed increasingly by Christians of all denominations. In Holy Week the two most widely observed occasions are Maundy Thursday, commemorating the institution of the Lord's Supper, and Good Friday, the commemoration of the Crucifixion. Services of Holy Communion are held in many, if not most churches, on Maundy Thursday, and the Three Hours' Service from noon until three o'clock in observance of the traditional hours of Christ's passion on the cross has come widely into vogue. Frequently meditations on the so-called seven last words from the cross are developed for such Good Friday services. The very extreme individualists who do not yet observe the festival of Easter Day are "few and far between" nowadays.

The problem about Easter no longer lies in any failure to observe Easter Sunday itself, but rather in our failure to observe Easter adequately as a *season* extending long after Easter Sunday and culminating in the glorious commemoration of our Lord's ascension. This will be discussed more fully in the next chapter, but here while we are thinking of Easter as a single Sunday, the climax of the preparatory Lenten weeks and of Passiontide, perhaps a brief introduction to Easter as a season is in order at this point.

Known to liturgists as "The Great Fifty Days," the period between Easter Sunday and Pentecost Sunday may well be made the most meaningful of the whole year, especially as one remembers that it was the resurrected Christ who became the central figure in the original Christian gospel. The good news that he arose from the dead *is* the gospel, is it not? Or at least is not the Resurrection what makes the gospel we preach a religion and not merely a philosophy? What a pity, then, that we compress into only one day, Easter Sunday, this greatest proclamation, when the ancient way of Christian teaching provided not only every Lord's Day, or Sunday, as a commemoration, but also the whole Eastertide and Ascensiontide sequence as periods for particular emphasis on the Resurrection!

The whole sequence leading up to Eastertide is characterized as "The Season of Renewal." At least the earlier part of the Lenten season, say up to Passion Sunday, provides the preacher with opportunity to treat almost any part of the general Christian message. In his book *Planning a Year's Pulpit Work*, Andrew W. Blackwood does not recommend any specific subject matter for Lenten preaching before Holy Week. Howard Chandler Robbins, in his *Preaching the Gospel*,[2] agrees that "in nonliturgical churches the preacher has greater freedom of selection; but he will be well advised to begin his course of sermons with the story of the temptation, as this is not only the historic beginning of Christ's ministry, but also the period in it which the forty days of Lent commemorate."

Ozora S. Davis, in his book previously mentioned, adds further to this general position in his statement, "Broadly considered, the preparation of the sermons for this period may begin profitably in the preacher's review of the meaning of these forty days of particular observance of private and public devotion in the experience of Christian people."

[2] Published by Harper and Brothers.

In other words, while Lent is especially a time for evangelistic preaching, there is no prescribed scriptural material which must be treated nor any one incident in Christ's life to be commemorated exclusively. Naturally, the doctrine of the Atonement will be emphasized during Lent, particularly in treating Christ's death and passion. Personal devotion and sacrifice will provide an underlying theme throughout the season. Candidates for church membership will be won and instructed in the Lenten preaching. A renewed consecration and dedication will be called for on the part of people who are already members. It is a period of concentrated religious emphasis, and whatever preaching will achieve the deepening of religious living is entirely appropriate to the Lenten season.

Probably most preachers find it challenging to develop a very special series or course of sermons for Lent. While this is by no means necessary, it does serve to heighten the importance of the season in the minds of the people and to lead them with increased interest from week to week through this preparatory season to the climax of Easter Day. My own Lenten preaching, as I look back on it, has had the widest range of subject matter and biblical selection, with particular attention to fundamental and familiar materials such as the twenty-third psalm, the Lord's Prayer, the Apostles' Creed, and the Ten Commandments. Even in evangelical or nonliturgical churches one's largest Sunday attendance is likely to be rallied during Lent which, it seems to me, should suggest basic scriptural and doctrinal materials for Lenten preaching. Lent is the only time many modern Americans will be regular churchgoers for any succession of Sundays. This is the time to build foundations for them.

Here, for example, is the form in which on the front of a Sunday bulletin I publicized one series of Lenten sermons, all from the great text John 3:16.

THE ANNUAL LENTEN SERMON SERIES

"The Gospel at its Greatest"
St. John iii:16

I. *God . . .*
February 23—"ON AFFIRMING THE INFINITE"

II. . . . *so loved . . .*
March 2—"THE SUPREME SO!"

III. . . . *the world . . .*
March 9—"THE WORK OF A WILL"

IV. . . . *that he gave . . .*
March 16—"ON GIVING GLORIOUSLY"

V. . . . *his only begotton Son . . .*
March 23 (Passion Sunday)
"GOD'S PARENTAL PASSION"

VI. . . . *that whosoever believeth in him . . .*
March 30 (Palm Sunday)
"THE CONDITION THAT CONVINCES"

VII. . . . *should not perish, but have everlasting life*
April 6 (Easter Sunday)
"A LIVING FAITH FOR A DYING AGE"

The following front cover of a Lenten bulletin will illustrate how by treating two of the Ten Commandments each Sunday for a series of five Sundays, I could also attach a Palm Sunday and an Easter Sunday sermon based on other scripture and at the same time maintain a connection calculated to carry the congregation's attention along throughout the seven weeks:

The
Lenten Season
1958

"The Eternal Laws of Life"

The Ten Commandments

Exodus xx:1-17

February 23: "You Can't Make Your Own God"
March 2: "The Sense of the Sacred"
March 9: "Life Must Go On"
March 16: "Hands Off!"
March 23: "The Neighborhood Fence"

"The Laws of Life Eternal"

Palm Sunday and Easter Sunday

St. Luke xix: 33-34

March 30: "Meeting Prior Claims"

I Corinthians xv: 22

April 6: "Suspended Sentence"

If Lent is the best of all seasons for series preaching, it has always seemed to me that it is equally the best of seasons for reviewing with one's people the most familiar Christian elements. This "Season of Renewal" is also a time for returning—for returning to the foundations of our faith. Calling the Lord's Prayer "The Pattern Prayer," I treated this most familiar of all our acts of worship this way as a Lenten series:

Who?	"Our Father . . ."
How?	"Hallowed . . ."
Whose?	"*Thy* kingdom . . . , *Thy* will . . ."
What?	"give us; . . . forgive us"
Where?	"lead us"
Why?	"for Thine is . . . the power"
When?	"for ever."

For another time I preached throughout Lent and on Easter Sunday from the scripture everybody knows by heart, the twenty-third psalm, calling the whole course "Faith at Its Finest." If a man may be permitted to judge his own work, I think the best Easter Sunday sermon I ever preached was in that series with the title "Surely!" from the last line of that psalm.

Mine—"The Lord is my shepherd."
Security Isn't Social—"He maketh me to lie down in green pastures, . . . beside still waters."
As Good as New—"He restoreth my soul."
My Goodness, for God's Sake—"He leadeth me in the paths of righteousness for his name's sake."
On Confronting Fear Frankly—"Yea, though I walk through the valley of the shadow of death, I will fear no evil."
Outfaced Foes—"Thou preparest a table before me in the presence of mine enemies." (Palm Sunday)
Surely!—"Surely goodness and mercy shall follow me all the days of my life: and I will dwell in the house of the Lord for ever." (Easter Sunday)

However, there is certainly no requirement that Lenten

preaching must treat only the familiar passages of scripture or frequently used devotional materials. Lloyd Douglas had recently published his best seller about Simon Peter when I tried a Lenten series connected only by the central character and called it "The Big Fisherman Finds His Faith." It went like this:

"From Sight to Insight"—Matt. 4:18, "And Jesus . . . saw Peter."

"That Sinking Feeling"—Matt. 14:29, 30, "And . . . Peter . . . beginning to sink, . . . cried, saying, Lord, save me."

"The Rebuke of Reality"—Matt. 16:23, "He . . . said unto Peter, . . . thou art an offence unto me."

"What's in It for Me?"—Matt. 19:27, "Then answered Peter and said unto him, Behold, we have forsaken all, and followed thee; what shall we have therefore?"

"So This Is the End?"—Matt. 26:58, "But Peter followed him afar off . . . and went in, and sat with the servants, to see the end."

"The Accent of Discipleship"—Matt. 26:73, "They that stood by, . . . said to Peter, Surely thou also art one of them; for thy speech bewrayeth thee."

"A Faith for the Fearful"—Mark 16:6-7, "Be not affrighted: Ye seek Jesus, . . . which was crucified: he is risen. . . . Go your way, tell . . . Peter."

A very deliberate departure from the familiar was a Lenten series one year entitled "Byways of His Last Days" which dealt with one of the casually mentioned incidents in the biblical account of each day of our Lord's last week, including a sermon on the possible reasons why there is no record of what happened to Jesus on the Wednesday of that week. The purpose of this group of sermons was not so much to strive for the unusual or original as to interest a congregation by being imaginative and even dramatic in making a penitent pilgrimage through Passiontide with Christ. Using any standard harmony of the Gospels in which the Synoptics and the Fourth Gospel are printed in parallel columns, one may bracket the record for each day of Christ's passion and select from each an abundance of sermon texts.

Another way I used of creating continuity in a sermon series for Lent was double-barreled: all the texts were taken from the Fourth Gospel, which made possible some teaching about that greatest Christian treatise, and there was also a thematic or connection title, "Our Spiritual Senses":

John 1:29—"A Sight That Saves"
John 4:31—"The Test of Taste"
John 2:24—"The Touch of Intuition"
John 8:9—"When the Heart Hears"
John 12:16—"Remembered Meanings"
John 15:26—"A Voice Victorious"

Alliteration, however much almost all preachers overwork it, can tie titles together tightly (how's that) for series purposes. Dr. E. Clayton Calhoun listed Lenten sermons this way: "Jesus, Minister to Men," "Jesus, Man of Mystery," "Jesus, Man of Mastery," and "Jesus, Master of Miracle." Dr. Charles Smythe did it thus: "The Fact of Jesus," "The Features of Jesus," "The Faith of Jesus," "The Field of Jesus," "The Fellowship of Jesus," and "The Fruitfulness of Jesus."

Once again let it be said, though, that Lenten preaching need not invariably be in series form. The season itself may well provide enough theme and connection. Early in Lent one may wish to call a congregation to the disciplines and devotions of the forty days by using the familiar Ps. 90:12—"So teach us to number our days, that we may apply our hearts unto wisdom." Another text with which to introduce Lent might be Rom. 12:1—"I beseech you therefore, brethren, by the mercies of God, that ye present your bodies a living sacrifice, holy, acceptable unto God."

For a Communion meditation in Lent here is a suggested text: Luke 15:2—"This man receiveth sinners, and eateth with them." For a Palm Sunday sermon, especially if people are to be prepared for a special Easter Sunday offering, the instructions Jesus gave his disciples about their Passover arrangements would offer a likely text: Matt. 21:3—"The Lord hath need of them." Two favorite Palm Sunday texts are: Matt. 21:10—"And when he was come into Jerusalem, all the city was moved, saying, Who is this?" and John 12:19—"Behold, the world is gone after him."

Passion Sunday offers special preaching values. It is possible on this occasion to treat the Atonement without being restricted to the crucifixion account alone. Such texts as these commend themselves for Passion Sunday preaching:

Matt. 27:25—"Then answered all the people and said, His blood be on us, and on our children."

Mark 15:3—"And the chief priests accused him of many things: but he answered nothing."

Matt. 27:13—"Hearest thou not how many things they witness against thee?"

John 18:31—"Take ye him, and judge him according to your law."

Maundy Thursday is observed almost exclusively with the Lord's Supper, and the accounts of the Last Supper are its standard preaching material, perhaps with I Cor. 11:20-

34 added to the records of the Gospels. The so-called "seven last words" are the equally traditional preaching material for Good Friday, but this need not be as invariably so. For Good Friday, especially for a Three Hours' Service, one might develop a series of meditations entitled "Characters of the Cross," discussing those who witnessed the Crucifixion or who participated in the passion of Christ: Caiaphas, Herod Antipas, Pilate, Simon the Cyrene, the Roman centurion, and others. Once I arranged sermons for a Three Hours' Service entitled "Words *to* the Cross," using not what Jesus said but what was said to him as he died. Another scheme for Good Friday preaching was called "The Four Points of the Cross": it points *down* into the earth in judgment upon the earth; it points *up* with aspirations to match our faith; it points sideways *there* toward our brothers waiting for redemption; it points sideways *here*; exactly toward us so that we cannot escape its meaning.

Nevertheless, the "seven last words" are useful and practical for Good Friday preaching. They easily permit a number of preachers to participate in a Three Hours' Service for one thing. They also can be arranged around a single theme. Dr. C. Wilson Sutton of New York City called the "words" promises of hope, for example, and listed them this way: "Our Hope of Pardon," "Our Hope of Heaven," "Our Hope of Understanding," "Our Hope of Victory," "Our Hope of Resurrection," "Our Hope of Achievement," and "Our Hope of Peace."

Based only on what may be surmised from the Easter Sunday sermon titles published in such profusion in newspapers on the Saturdays before, I have been wondering how much of the *Christian* doctrine of the Resurrection is being preached in evangelical churches on Easter. Do today's preachers need reminding that the Christian proclamation on Easter Sunday is more than the idea of *survival* of ancient paganism and modern spiritualism and more than the *immortality* of Greek, Roman, and Teutonic mythology? Surely the teaching of Christianity is the resurrection of the *dead* to *life* everlasting. The distinctions are important and basic even if they cannot be delineated here. At any rate, here are texts for sermons which will make the Christian differentiation:

Job 14:14—"If a man die, shall he live again?"

I Cor. 15:12—"Now if Christ be preached that he rose from the dead, how say some among you that there is no resurrection of the dead?"

Ps. 39:7—"And now, Lord, what wait I for? my hope is in thee."

Col. 3:3—"For ye are dead, and your life is hid with Christ in God."

Eph. 1:19-20—"His power [is] to us-ward, . . . the . . . mighty power, which he wrought in Christ, when [God] raised him from the dead."

II Cor. 5:4—"For we that are in this tabernacle do groan, being burdened: not for that we would be unclothed, but clothed upon, that mortality might be swallowed up of life."

Naturally and rightly the Gospel accounts of the Resurrection will provide most of the Easter Sunday preaching material for Christian preachers. You might find it interesting to combine these two texts to relate the Crucifixion with the Resurrection: Matt. 27:51—"And the earth did quake, and the rocks rent," and Matt. 28:2—"And, behold, there was a great earthquake." Let a reverent imagination work on that and see what develops. If your church uses Easter Sunday for an important missionary offering, as many do, here's a text, Matt. 28:8—"And they departed quickly from the sepulchre with fear and great joy; and did run to bring his disciples word." The unexpected visit of Jesus at eventide after the awful events of the first Easter Day, recorded in John 20:19, offers an especially appropriate scripture for an evening sermon on an Easter Sunday.

When all is said, a real preacher needs less human guidance during the progression from Ash Wednesday through Easter Sunday than for any other portion of the Church Year. For the meaning and message of this a preacher must first experience it for himself, vitally and vibrantly, for here is represented most of what is *distinctive* about Christianity. More of the Hebraic is in the messianic context of Advent and Christmastide, more of the apostolic in the atmosphere of Epiphanytide, and more of the prophetic in Kingdomtide. But the Lenten-Passiontide-Eastertide-Whitsuntide sequence, some of which will be treated in a separate chapter, speaks the pure and personal gospel of Christ himself. Once all this has been heard in one's own heart, no preacher can contain all the words and ways that come to him by which his own insights can be shared with his people. Measureless variety and endless invention await a preacher's call during this period. He can hardly avoid preaching the best of Christianity's meaning through Lent or scarcely escape being at his sermonic best approaching Easter. This is the time each year when the humblest parson is a "great preacher," for he is preaching the gospel at its greatest.

Eastertide, the Great Fifty Days

Liturgical scholars of various communions have come to call the period which commemorates Christ's postresurrection experiences on earth "The Great Fifty Days." This is the same as Eastertide, which includes the days until the anniversary of Christ's ascension; but since Ascension Day always comes on a Thursday and as such is seldom observed by evangelical Protestants until the Sunday following, if at all, and since the Pentecost message of Whitsunday, a week after Ascension Sunday, has such a close connection in significance as well as in sequence with both Christ's resurrection and his ascension, we may practically regard "The Great Fifty Days" as a relative term and use it to designate the whole progression of Eastertide, Ascensiontide, and Whitsunday.

The rediscovery of the traditional Calendar by contemporary evangelical churches is one of the developments I have witnessed in my own generation. I can recall when it was prudent to use the phrase "Pre-Easter" instead of "Lent" if one would avoid stirring up the sensibilities of many church people. Two decades later, as I write this, Lent is almost universally observed in the churches of America. At least, it is no longer a suspicious word. The Protestant pastor who now commends Lent as a useful church season is no longer suspected of having put on the pope's petticoats.

Of course, the progression of appreciation for the Church Year has not been uniform. It is more observed in some places than in others, and more of it is observed in some places than in others. If Lent is now emphasized in most churches, Advent is used slightly less, and the seasons after Easter Sunday receive least attention of all.

If we were consistent in being evangelical churchmen, this season, the Great Fifty Days, would be our favorite. If we are going to observe *any* of the traditional Calendar, this is the period with which our free churches should feel the closest affinity. If we claim that our churchmanship is rooted in the practices of the primitive Church of the New Testament, this is the period to remember that Church's beginnings. If the witness of the Spirit and the empowerings of pentecostal experience are still our great doctrines and declarations, this is the time of year when our denominations can make their special emphasis in every community. If any one of us is bothered by borrowing Lenten customs from older communions or feels accused of imitating the liturgical churches when we have the Lord's Supper on Maundy Thursday or a Three Hours' Service on Good Friday, the Eastertide-through-Ascensiontide-to-Pentecost period is a natural, ready-made time to be as Protestant as we please, as evangelical and biblical as we know how. This season is *our* time at bat. This is when we can get in our best licks.

For our purposes it is a fortunate fact that May 24,

Aldersgate Day, always comes within this period. Its proximity to, and occasionally its coincidence with, Pentecost Sunday serves evangelical churchmanship well regardless of denomination. An increasing number of annual denominational meetings are being scheduled during the late spring weeks. This all adds special significance to the Great Fifty Days. A general impression is that more pastoral changes take place in the spring and early summer than at any other time of year; so look at the summary which has been added so reverently to Mark's Gospel in the closing verse, Mark 16:20—"And they went forth, and preached every where, the Lord working with them, and confirming the word with signs following. Amen." This is part of the scripture which belongs to the season following Easter Sunday and is, therefore, an appropriate text in its own right for this period of sending and calling preachers. Or, if practical parish considerations indicate such a need, the scripture of this season also includes Luke 24:53—"And were continually in the temple, praising and blessing God. Amen," which describes the fervor not only of the first Christians but also of the pioneer American evangelicals; offers an opportunity to emphasize continuity of worship; and like the Markan text, has a concluding "amen" to suggest what ought to be the response of present-day disciples.

I can think of two reasons why our evangelical denominations have not made the most of the Great Fifty Days. One grows out of that interaction of the secular and the sacred which characterizes so much of our American culture. This makes us jump the gun, tempts us to start using up the values of Easter before Eastertide arrives. It is even more true of Christmas, but true enough about the American observance of Easter, that for weeks ahead the shop windows and advertisements and all the commercial promotion culminate on Easter Sunday to such a degree that any Eastertide emphasis after that one first day seems anticlimatic. It is hard enough to make Lent meaningful in the face of commercial bombardments about Easter clothes, candies, hats, and hams; it is even harder to proceed from Easter Sunday into the season of Easter*tide* without the support of a secular society which supposes that after the first Sunday Easter is over for another year and that the next big religious-commercial date will be Mother's Day.

The other reason which occurs to me for our Protestant failure to take fullest spiritual advantage of this season is theological. Eric Baker in his little book *Preaching Theology*, written mainly for British preachers, points out this failure to indoctrinate. He says:

> The doctrine of the Ascension of our Lord does not usually receive the attention it deserves. We have noticed how many church-goers pass from Palm Sunday to Easter with no public acknowledgment of Good Friday. But it may be fairly urged that at any rate they know about Good Friday. . . . When it comes, however, to Ascension Day, which always falls on a Thursday, it is to be feared that a large proportion of practicing Free Churchmen allow the festival to pass entirely unnoticed. Nor is the omission by any means corrected invariably on the following Sunday. This is a great pity, as the doctrine of the Ascension should be to us a real source of comfort and of strength.

Well, at least this fault is not exclusively American!

But it is a pity, indeed, that we use up all our preaching capital about our Lord's resurrection on a single day each year. And it is an added pity that we do not help our people see the vital connection between Christ's resurrection and his ascension. The appearances of Christ after his resurrection lead naturally to that final, unique manifestation we call his ascension. It not only was his last earthly appearance, but the disciples knew that it was his last. Instead of sorrowing over his separation from them they rejoiced, for they had realized that he would be with them more really and perfectly from then on than he ever could be in the flesh. Baker puts it succinctly,

> So for us the Ascension might be termed the festival of the unseen but real world. No fact is more important than that the unseen things are the real things. . . . The most wonderful things in life are not the things we can see or touch, weigh or measure, the most wonderful and the most real things are the unseen values such as truth, friendship, goodness and love.

We ought to use the Great Fifty Days to lead our people every year from a first long look at the visible, actual, risen Christ of Easter Sunday through the scripture accounts about his Eastertide appearances, and on to the ascended triumph of his even more real, though now invisible, presence with God the Father, and then finally to the abiding presence of both Father and Son with every believer who receives the witness of the Holy Spirit poured out at Pentecost. From the empty tomb of Joseph's garden to the company tarrying at Jerusalem for a promised empowering is a dramatic progression of the biblical record—and a "great fifty days" for preaching!

After your best possible sermon on Easter Sunday from the main gospel record of the Resurrection try some of these texts on succeeding Sundays:

Matt. 28:15 contrasted with Luke 24:8—"You Can't Forget Easter." Even a doubting, disbelieving world has been changed by the Resurrection, however much the doctrine is explained away—"This saying is commonly reported among the Jews until this day." For those who believe, it adds meaning and purpose to all Christian teaching—"They remembered his words" after his resurrection. All ethical concepts, all social betterment, all individual holiness have greater significance because of Christ's resurrection or lesser significance if they ignore that resurrection. Take it from there.

Mark 16:14-16—"The Damnation of Disbelief." Here's strong language for a prophetic spirit. If Jesus "upbraided them with their unbelief and hardness of heart" after his resurrection, it may well be that modern preachers need to say some hard, strong things about attitudes and actions which amount practically to unbelief about the life to come. Does preaching still bring hearers "under conviction of sin"? This scripture ought to do just that.

Matt. 28:16—"His Last Mountain." If you aren't a prophet, maybe you're a poet. Jesus had been on a mountain to preach the greatest sermon of all time, later on a Mount of Transfiguration, and even on a Mount Calvary before he came to that last unknown hill in Galilee "into a mountain" where he had appointed his disciples to meet him. Yet still some worshiped him, but some doubted him. He must be lifted even higher in his ascension before he can claim the faith of all.

Luke 24:19 contrasted with Luke 24:49—"The Prophet Who Promised Power." A "prophet mighty" was all they could say about Jesus until they recognized his resurrection. Unlike all the prophets who went before him, Jesus could "send the promise of my Father upon you" confidently and create a whole new religious value which we call Christianity.

Luke 24:32—"A Preview of Pentecost" describes that inner burning of spiritual fires which Pentecost later brought to all the disciples and to all who have received the Holy Spirit in generations following. It is the voice of Jesus talking with us along the way of life and the testimony of scriptural truth which still enables us to feel our hearts "strangely warmed," to use Wesley's immortal phrase.

Luke 24:36-37—"The Peace That Frightens at First." When Jesus stands in the midst of man's confusion offering peace, the world is usually frightened at first. Peace does seem ghostly, unreal, even at first unnatural, if not impossible. The conditions of peace shake and challenge so many present arrangements.

To these texts may be added many more from the Fourth Gospel's extensive record of the postresurrection appearances of Christ. The epistles contain numerous references to the risen Lord and by no means should be neglected in Ascensiontide. To the Acts, of course, we look mainly in preaching about Pentecost, but the doctrine of the Holy Spirit and the doctrine of the Church are abundantly supported by other New Testament writings. Since references to the Holy Spirit are so pervasive of the whole Bible, it is hard to imagine that on Pentecost Sunday once each year any preacher would need help here in finding suitable scripture or textual material for Whitsunday sermons. The second chapter of the Acts, like the Christmas story in Luke's second chapter, is a spring of sermonic inspiration which never runs dry though preachers return to it year and year after year. Occasionally some coincidence of dates may present a preaching problem, however. For example, when Pentecost Sunday and National Family Week coincide, you might need this abridgment of Acts 2:17—"Saith God, I will pour out of my Spirit upon . . . your sons and your daughters."

When the Calendar was first developing, they called Pentecost "Whitsunday" from the white robes the catechumens wore on this principal baptismal occasion. That great feast of the Holy Spirit, that anniversary of the Church's birthday, might still be made a climactic ingathering for every church's fall-winter-spring working year. At least we ought not to permit the well-known summer slump to begin always until *after* Whitsunday. Far too many congregations are permitted that unwarranted luxury much too soon after Easter Sunday. Is this because we preachers have neglected the Great Fifty Days as a time for great preaching about a great gospel? If so, let's start making this season evangelical Christianity's greatest climax. Let's claim it for our own. Peculiarly and particularly it belongs to our kind of religion.

Trinitytide and Kingdomtide

THE SUMMER AND THE FALL, OR THE WEEKS BETWEEN Pentecost Sunday and Advent, taken together, constitute about half of each year, depending somewhat on the variable date of Easter Sunday. As has been explained in the previous chapter, what is sometimes called "The Great Fifty Days" culminates on Ascension Day but really climaxes in Whitsuntide or Pentecost Sunday. This Sunday, whether called Whitsunday or Pentecost Sunday, interchangeable terms, is followed by the only occasion of the Church Year named for a specific doctrine, Trinity Sunday, which in turn introduces a long succession of weeks through the summer, Trinitytide. The older and more liturgical communions continue to designate as Sundays "after Trinity" all that come in the autumn as well until the "Sunday next before Advent" near the end of November. It is equally correct to use Pentecost Sunday instead of Trinity Sunday to begin this whole system of counting Sundays, and indeed this is highly recommended by some liturgical purists. Thus, one could designate the same Sunday either as "the twelfth Sunday after Trinity" or as "the thirteenth

Sunday after Pentecost." Trinity Sunday itself did not find its way as such into the Calendar until the fourteenth century, which is rather late as these things go. Probably this is why some experts in liturgics prefer the older form "after Pentecost" instead of "after Trinity," the former being far more ancient.

Whether the long sequence of Sundays stretching through the summer and fall from Pentecost Sunday until Advent are called Trinitytide, or whether they are designated as the "first, second, third, and so forth, Sunday after Pentecost," or whether they are listed as the "first, second, third, and so forth, Sunday in Whitsuntide, or whether the fall Sundays are separated from one of these seasons and given the separate name Kingdomtide really makes little difference. Sundays and seasons are liturgically of three kinds: festivals, fasts, and *ferial.* The last term means only that an occasion is neither feast nor fast, and the point here is that most of the Sundays after Trinity, or in Trinitytide, or after Pentecost, or in Whitsuntide, or in all of them *plus* Kingdomtide, are simply ferial. They do not suggest any special festivity other than that every Sunday is an anniversary of Christ's resurrection, nor any more penitential solemnity than that all Christian worship is confessional. A preacher may well be following the Calendar during this whole period while he ranges widely through the Scriptures for texts or when he treats sermonically many, many different aspects of the Christian religion. Unless he is being guided by a lectionary, a preacher is free from direction by the Calendar for all except a few Sundays.

Yet even though specific themes and subjects are not indicated for the summer weeks, much less prescribed, there is certainly a difference between summertime preaching and that of other seasons which most ministers recognize. While I don't wish to imply that summer preaching must be in series form, the following outlines of some summer series may illustrate what I mean.

SUPPERS FOR OUR SOULS

"Life's Menu"—Luke 10:42 (Moffatt), "Mary has chosen the best dish."

"Balanced Diet"—Prov. 30:8 (A.S.V.),

"Give me neither poverty nor riches;
Feed me with the food that is needful for me."

"Choice of Dessert"—Isa. 7:15, "Butter and honey shall he eat, that [the child] may know to refuse the evil, and choose the good."

THE GROWING SEASON

Rom. 11:16—"If the root be holy, so are the branches."

Hos. 14:4—"He shall grow as the lily."

Ps. 1:3—"He shall be like a tree . . . that bringeth forth his fruit in his season."

In other words, summer is a season for some variety, some imagination, some popularity in your preaching, if you don't take this to mean that those characteristics are exclusively summerish. I guess what I'm trying to say is that summer is a good time for the light touch.

However, summer may also be an excellent time for some series preaching from certain books or sections of the Bible. For example, some of the major messages of the minor prophets might produce an interesting and instructive summer sequence. One year I preached on the book of Job with the general title "Dealing with Trouble," which went like this:

"Trouble Is Really Normal"—Job 5:7, "Man is born unto trouble, as the sparks fly upward."
"Resentment Won't Help for Long"—Job 31:29-30 (Moffatt), "If ever I . . . practised the sweet sin of cursing, . . ."
"Try Standing off and Looking at Your Trouble"—Job 5:8, Were I in your place, "I would seek unto God."
"Face the Worst That Could Happen?"—Job 14:14, "If a man die, shall he live again?"

Among other books with which I have dealt homiletically in summer seasons are Genesis, Revelation, and Psalms. There is some advantage, especially in summer, in preaching on biblical material with which people either have a general familiarity already or about which they have at least some curiosity.

Another Bible series for summer preaching was one I attempted from the brief New Testament letters: I Peter, a discussion of Christian faith which can endure if the Church ever goes underground again; Jude, a consideration of the problems which arise when the Church comes of age, becomes less enthusiastic and mature; Philemon, an emphasis on the continuing importance of an individual in a steadily growing Christianity; and II Peter, a treatment of the Church's need to rethink its faith in each succeeding generation as conditions change. I believe that people can be encouraged to study and read a book of the Bible or a section of the Scriptures as a special summer devotion when a minister arranges his preaching this way.

Is your church conditioned originally to a revival each

year, and are you finding it harder and harder to get interest and attendance in a week of daily services? Have you ever considered announcing "Six Sundays of Revival" (or four, or eight) during a summer season in lieu of the same number of week-night services? I know of a number of places where this has become a standard use of the summer season, and I tried this once myself in a church which I served in Virginia. I found it to be a fairly satisfactory substitute for a preaching mission, and I'm certain that better attendance was achieved and that the summer is time to do this if it is going to be done at all. I preached on "The Working Words of Our Faith," though I don't offer this as an outline of systematic theology:

"Grace"—Eph. 2:8, "By grace are ye saved . . . ; it is the gift of God."

"Conversion"—Matt. 18:3, "Except ye be converted, and become as little children, ye shall not enter into the kingdom of heaven."

"Holiness"—Gen. 17:1, "I am the Almighty God; walk before me, and be thou perfect."

"Atonement"—I John 2:2, "He is the propitiation for our sins."

"Salvation"—Ps. 3:8, "Salvation belongeth unto the Lord."

Another summer, illness in my family prevented me from taking any vacation, so I did what I had wanted to do for a long time—gave all the Sundays for a full two-month period to a training course in churchmanship for adults. It went like this:

For the living of these days,

For the saving of our times,
The Church must be—
Doctrinally Sound,
Evangelistically Passionate,
Efficiently Organized,
Liturgically Inspiring,
An Adequate Fellowship,
Socially Concerned,
Spiritually Effective,
And Eternally Established

What I have tried to show is that the summer season is a very useful one within the Church Year, that it has its own flavor, its own values, and that it offers a certain relief following the more carefully defined seasons which precede it.

I have already commented on Pentecost Sunday or Whitsunday as it may be tied to the Great Fifty Days. Trinity Sunday, always a week later, is also an occasion for some emphasis on spiritual experience, especially on the doctrine of the Trinity, and both are like most other single occasions in the Calendar whose themes are more or less obvious and which really need little striving after variety. Nothing is likely to become seriously monotonous which is repeated no more often than once a year.

Another special Sunday which comes every summer, though not an ecclesiastical observance, is that which is nearest the Fourth of July. Patriotism undoubtedly will demand and probably deserve some recognition on this occasion.

Now let's talk about Kingdomtide. It is the newest addition to the Calendar and is almost wholly an American innovation. It may turn out to be a mainly Free Church appellation, for the more conservative and liturgical bodies seem not to have adopted it to any great extent, possibly because they have more mechanics such as official prayer books, ornaments and vestmental rubrics, and so forth, to change if they separate the summer and fall seasons.

Kingdomtide was proposed in 1937 by the former Federal Council of Churches, and has been accepted by the present National Council of Churches. The Methodist Church included it in all seasonal sequences of *The Book of Worship* which was first published in 1946. Other denominations are experiencing some use of it, though perhaps the general acceptance of Kingdomtide has been slow in coming. Paul E. Holdcraft in his booklet *Texts and Themes for the Christian Year* feels that the observance is definitely increasing when he comments on Kingdomtide.

At any rate, Kingdomtide is a very valuable period indeed. It begins the last Sunday in August with an occasion called the Festival of Christ the King. That occasion itself is not likely to be observed generally in evangelical Protestantism for a long, long time to come, if ever. Its name is what's wrong with it for Protestants. It sounds like what our fathers called "popery," whether it really connotes that or not. But that doesn't prevent Kingdomtide from commending itself as a season.

For one thing, there is an important change in psychological atmosphere in the autumn as well as a difference between summer and fall temperatures, and churches reflect this. Sunday attendance steps up, activities and programs take on new pace, and the fall seems to demand a new seasonal emphasis different from the one which may have dragged through a hot summer. For another consideration, some of the specific observances which always come in the autumn deal with the great issues of Christ's kingdom, and this relationship ought to be made manifest. There is Labor Day Sunday, Reformation Sunday, Temperance Sunday, and World Peace Sunday coming within Kingdomtide. And there is the Church's glorious memorial observance, All Saints' Day, and also Thanksgiving Day, which adds religion to patriotism better than does any other occasion. Since most evangelical churches and preachers observe most of these special occasions anyhow, the broader term Kingdomtide might as well be used for any additional values it may offer.

One such value is the definite emphasis on the social concerns of Christianity which Kingdomtide calls for. As they have increasingly demanded the attention of Christians in modern times, they deserve a recognized place in the Calendar. Moreover, it may help a preacher to speak prophetically about social issues if it is realized that he is doing so not only truthfully but also *appropriately*. The use of Kingdomtide not only ensures that social concern will not be lost from a preaching schedule but also helps secure congregational attention by adding the interest inherent in a seasonable observance, especially if that observance is well planned and promoted.

However, Kingdomtide does not lend itself well to series preaching. Several Sundays in Kingdomtide, as listed in a previous paragraph, call for special observance, and they are spotted here and there so irregularly throughout the season that they likely would interrupt any sermon series.

A good text with which to introduce Kingdomtide, to

help people anticipate its continuity and to apreciate its importance, is Matt. 4:23—"Jesus went about . . . preaching . . . the kingdom." The kingdom parables will be a fruitful biblical source for Kingdomtide sermons, and maybe even more so will be the Prophets, especially Amos, Micah, and Hosea.

For Labor Day Sunday, the first in September, is suggested the text John 6:27—"Labour not for the meat which perisheth, but for that . . . which endureth unto everlasting life," or a fragment from Mic. 7:3—"With both hands earnestly . . . ." Another text for this occasion might be I Cor. 10:31—"Whatsoever ye do, do all to the glory of God." Some of the problems organized labor is having might suggest the use of Gen. 15:11—"And when birds of prey came down, . . . Abram drove them away." (R.S.V.)

Near the end of each October most Protestant churches will observe Reformation Sunday, probably as a union affair with other congregations. Of course, the classic text for a sermon on this occasion is Rom. 1:17—"The just shall live by faith." It is probably far more effective to be positive about Protestantism than to be merely negative about Romanism, and one might even accord fullest recognition to the gains for Christianity which undoubtedly are preserved by Roman Catholicism before asserting the advances of Protestantism. If that is true, here's a text for the purpose: I Cor. 12:31—"And yet shew I unto you a more excellent way." Other Reformation Sunday texts might be these:

Ps. 22:4-5—"Our fathers trusted in thee . . . and were not confounded."

I Kings 21:3—"The Lord forbid it me, that I should

give [away] the inheritance of my fathers," being sure to include both our Protestant *and* our Roman inheritance.

The question of authority between Protestantism and Roman Catholicism might be dealt with from the text Luke 20:2—"Who is he that gave thee this authority?"

World Temperance Sunday comes near the end of October and is a legitimate emphasis of Kingdomtide. Since Christian education is more and more the approach of the churches to the alcohol problem, this fragmentary text, II Pet. 1:6, might be useful: "And to knowledge, temperance . . . ." A classic temperance message is the one many preachers have based on the account of Noah's drunkenness when the flood had subsided, but it might have special contemporary significance if given this treatment: When the violence of nature which the Bible calls a flood had subsided, a fresh new world awaited new moral leadership, but Noah only got drunk. In the lull we had following the devastating World War II we were given the opportunity to achieve new moral values before the bombs and missiles could bring more complete annihilation. Couldn't we do better than Noah, or was there still to be just drunkenness?

A subseason within Kingdomtide is All Saints' season. The day itself is November 1, but evangelical Protestants will more likely observe it on the first Sunday in November. And observe it they should. If we have canceled the saints out, one by one, as far as their ancient places in the Calendar are concerned, the least we can do is recognize them altogether once a year; or are sainthood and saintliness no longer of concern to evangelicals? It's strange that the Holiness bodies have overlooked All Saints' Sunday. It would seem to be a "natural" for them.

Of course, Protestantism defines saints in the New Testament sense and has never officially canonized any since. But the saints of God, many of unremembered names, have lived in every generation of the Church's history. Haven't you known one or two? And all the Church are potential saints, for that is our faith in Christ's redemptive power.

All Saints' and Memorial Sunday are really interchangeable terms in the language of the Church. The occasion is indeed the best of all memorial occasions, and the annual observance of All Saints' Sunday that way obviates funeral sermons and elegies from time to time all through a year. It has been my own practice and that of many pastors to announce the names on All Saints' Sunday of all who have died during the year past and to preach with some relationship to their deaths. This need be neither morbid nor funereal.

Here are some All Saints' Sunday texts in that vein:

Rev. 14:13, "Blessed are the dead which die in the Lord."
Num. 23:10, "Let me die the death of the righteous."
Heb. 11:13, "These all died in faith."

From the passage Rev. 7:9-17 will arise the whole message of All Saints' Sunday with the clear Christian accent on triumph and victory.

World Peace Sunday in mid-November arises from the patriotic occasion formerly known as Armistice Day. The Christian preacher who cannot convert the latter to the former is rare today, thank God. He will feel often on this occasion that he is another Jeremiah (6:14), crying "Peace, peace; when there is no peace," but Kingdomtide will not pass without his trying to cry peace. He may proclaim to those who have changed Armistice Day to Veterans' Day the words of the psalmist (120:7), "I am for peace: but when I speak, they are for war." Nevertheless, his message on World Peace Sunday must continue to be the words of Job (22:21), "Acquaint now thyself with [God] and be at peace."

Finally, Kingdomtide will come each year to Thanksgiving time. This admixture of historical patriotism and dutiful praise, duly enabled by act of Congress and proclaimed in annual documents by whichever assistants to presidents and governors happen to have the most florid literary style during any current political administration is nearly the hardest quasi-Church occasion to make meaningful of all the Calendar. It will compete with football games, hunting seasons, and turkey dinners not always with much success. I have preached my share of sermons about fruitful harvests to urban congregations who couldn't care less and even about the first Yankee Pilgrims to dear people in Virginia completely dubious that any good thing could really arise in New England. Frankly, the only Thanksgiving sermon which gave me, at least, much satisfaction was from the text Jer. 8:20—"The harvest is past, the summer is ended, and we are not saved." The next best, I thought, was from the account in Luke 17 about the nine lepers who forgot to come back and say thanks.

Nevertheless, Kingdomtide as a whole is an enjoyable season for me as a preacher. I'm glad for the change of pace it brings each autumn, relieved not to work with closely related series for a time, and sure that my people need the impact of a concentrated concern with social, even controversial, issues. The Protestant pulpit is still a force for social reformation, maybe never more so than now. Any year's preaching which lacks considerable social content seriously fails to proclaim the whole gospel. I like Kingdomtide, and I believe the Church needs it.

Using the Church Year for Planning

My father and my uncle, when they were boys, went squirrel hunting. Uncle shot two long before my father shot any, and swaggered a bit with his two trophies slung over his shoulder.

"How's for lettin' me carry one of them?" pled my father, anxious for even vicarious glory.

"Every feller totes his own squirrels!" was the adamant refusal, and Uncle proceeded to shoot even more squirrels while his younger brother still got none at all. The hunt ranged farther and farther afield, the hours of walking began to drag, and the autumn sun got hotter at midday. When at last a dozen or more squirrels literally began to make their dead weight felt, Uncle suggested that maybe after all he could share some of his Nimrod's glory.

"Here, Bud," he offered with new generosity, "you can carry some of these squirrels 'cause you haven't shot any yourself."

"Every feller totes his own squirrels!" was the classic

justice of my father's reply. For two generations it served as one of those family sayings every household has.

That's how it is with preaching plans. Every fellow has his own. The only valid test is whether he carries it or it carries him. Any plan that becomes cumbersome or too involved isn't worth much and soon takes the joy out of preaching.

As I pointed out in a paragraph or two at the opening of this book, the Church Calendar provides a relatively simple program for planning each year's preaching. It is sufficiently fixed and sufficiently flexible, and in this chapter I hope I can amplify and detail the Calendar's values as a preaching plan.

First, it is fixed enough to make long-range planning and filing possible. The days and seasons of the Church Year repeat and return and can be anticipated. Thus it isn't necessary to wait until the department store show-windows are filled with Christmas decorations to discover that Christmas is coming. You can plan for Christmas months ahead—or for Easter or Ascensiontide or World Peace Sunday or Thanksgiving or any of the fixed occasions of the Calendar. It is helpful that about half of any year's preaching can be known in advance.

That is like the liberty a known route affords a traveler. One is free to plan a trip because the way and its landmarks have been mapped and may be known in advance. Assuming one has some destination in mind, there is more real freedom in traveling a well-built highway than in hacking out a wilderness trail across uncharted distances. A pioneer may have the satisfactions of endeavor, but I doubt if he has much free time to look at the scenery, or even to take an occasional sidetrip. He must stay too busy finding his way. The steady progression of the Calendar is marked year by year with the recurring mileposts and landmarks of its fixed days and seasons. There are great freedom and real liberty for the preacher who follows its ancient roadway. He knows where he is and where he is going. So, soon, do his hearers.

Actually, far more flexibility is found in the Church Year than may be commonly supposed. For one thing, nearly half of the Sundays of the Calendar are "after Trinity" or are in the weeks of Kingdomtide when special themes are not necessarily indicated. The widest range of preaching is not only possible but is also appropriate, for what elements of divinity are not within the proper purview of God's fatherhood, sonship, and Holy Spirit? Or is there any gospel emphasis not related in some way to the vast concept of God's kingdom? The preacher who has some special subject on his chest (or in his barrel) can almost always find an unclaimed Sunday in Trinitytide or Kingdomtide when he can plan for that single message.

Even more significant, however, is the way the seemingly fixed themes of Calendar occasions admit the widest variety of treatment. Lent, for example, is the prime season for developing the spiritual devotion and moral discipline of Christians, in the light of the Cross or under the shadow of its judgment. This means that Lenten preaching may be intensely pietistic or broadly social, for what is larger in scope than the message of redemption? There are Lenten sermons in every section of Scripture, and almost infinite invention is prompted by the penitential observance of Lent. The point is that the doctrines or Scriptural events which correspond with days and periods in the Calendar are always related to the whole Christian revelation and thus need not be narrowly defined or repetitiously treated year after year.

Moreover, it is frequently possible to combine the themes of occasions with the special needs of a parochial program. Suppose, for example, that there is clearly need for stewardship cultivation within a congregation which during a certain winter is beginning a building enterprise or approaching a financial campaign. The whole Nativity sequence of Advent, Christmastide, and Epiphanytide lends its basic theme to support the pastor's preaching:

> In Advent he will remind his people that Christ's coming requires an accounting by his stewards, that Christ's judgment is upon our use of what God has created, that Christ's kingdom is to be established materially on earth as it is spiritually in heaven. In Christmastide he will make effective use of the real meaning of the Incarnation, that God so loved the world that he gave just as Christians so love God that they give.
>
> And during the Epiphany season, he surely will find stewardship applications suggested by the Wise Men and their gifts.

This whole balance then between the fixity and the flexibility of the Calendar is what makes it a workable vehicle for planned preaching, and these are some of the answers to a first resistance by ministers of Free Church background who have taken for granted that the Church Calendar is part of the rigidity of the liturgical denominations. Isn't it all too true that the evangelical churchman who insists he must be free to preach God's immediate inspirations usually seems to get them only on Saturday nights? At least his people may often think so. And if the only alternative is some organized program of planning and preparation, then what is more proven by the developing devotion of the Christian ages and by the devout disciplines of the Church's centuries than is the Calendar? It is not only a workable plan but a worthy one. God has blessed it in the life of his Church and still does.

The actual procedure for planning a preaching program on the basis of the Church Year would not differ greatly from the way a preacher forecasts his pulpit work in any other context. That is to say, some of the planning would naturally begin with ideas, themes, subjects, topics, and texts already in mind or already accumulated, and some would require casting about for appropriate materials. How and where a preacher gets his sermonic suggestions originally and how he keeps or classifies them varies with each man. My own method is as simple as dropping clippings, notes, and scriptural references in the drawer of a desk and leaving them there until an annual sorting and sifting which usually comes during the so-called vacation season —but, "Every fellow totes his own squirrels!"

Since, however, a principal and perhaps unique advantage of using the Calendar is that it makes possible a whole year's plan, whether the entire year is scheduled at one time or whether each approaching season is planned as a unit from time to time during a year, this is a procedure which will work, I believe, for most preachers:

On work sheets first list the days and seasons of the Church Year with their corresponding civil dates, Sunday by Sunday. If evening services are held, space for both morning and evening sermons needs to be allowed. A few weekway dates probably must be inserted in their proper places, such as Thanksgiving Day, Christmas Eve or Christmas Day, or any occasions when a sermon will be needed for other than Sundays. For each date on the schedule should be added any notes indicating denominational or parochial emphases or observances. For example, the Sunday after Ascension Day may be the Sunday when one's conference, synod, or association will be in session. That should be noted. Or a Sunday in Eastertide may be the congregation's annual pledge day for the coming year's budget. Trinity Sunday may come in June when the church school usually observes Children's Day. There will be some of these combinations of occasions in every year's plan. Each such special circumstance should be forecast and indicated.

Now from the desk drawer or from wherever thoughts and themes, titles and texts, have been hoarded, bring forth all the sermon ideas previously stored and start the process of putting them into the Calendar. Some, maybe much, of the material will prove to be unworthy and unwanted after the critical and objective second look which their hibernation now permits. A wastebasket is the most important item of furniture in a preacher's study!

But out of the pile comes an idea, maybe a barest notion, which promises a fine missionary sermon. Slot it for an Epiphany Sunday. Here is a text on the subject of prayer. Preach it as a single sermon on a ferial Sunday in Trinitytide? Or tie it in with a Lenten series? Still another note is pulled out of the pile which suggests a fine sermon for Trinity Sunday but won't quite fit the theme of Children's Day which happens to coincide with that date. Observe

Trinity Sunday at the evening service and give the morning hour to Children's Day? Put the good Trinity Sunday note away for another year? Slot it for the first Sunday after Trinity? Would the sonship and fatherhood of God on Trinity Sunday suggest a parent-child theme for Children's Day? So the process of discard and decision proceeds until all the possibilities of one's stack or store have been dealt with, each put where it seems to belong, either in the trash box or opposite one of the dates in the coming Church Year.

Probably it is a work of supererogation for one preacher to suggest to others that some use may be made of old sermons in planning any new course of preaching. All of us do this and not without advantage to our people. Many a sermon grows and glows as it is reworked from time to time. It may well prove true, moreover, that a sermon once attempted without complete success will do far better when it is adapted to another occasion. The text paraphrased, "If I be lifted up from the earth, [I] will draw all men unto me," seemed to me at first to be perfect for Ascensiontide use, but it never quite fired until years later I tried it in Passiontide. I then realized that it is much more truly related to our Lord's crucifixion than to his ascension. Sermon notes from a previous pastorate are not to be swept aside lightly. So to the new material now integrated with a Church Year schedule, add any useful material from accumulated sermon files, and at least a few more dates may be planned.

But only the unusual man will find his dates all planned at this point. He is either unusually brilliant or unusually uncritical of his own thoughts. For most, now comes the time for invention, imagination, and inspiration. After using what has come to hand, now is the time to start digging! Or call it being creative.

Now this is when the Church Year itself comes to the rescue. Even with those blank dates staring you in the face, it's still not so much a question of *what* to preach about as it is *how* best to preach the themes of an ancient sequence which add up to the whole gospel of Christ. In other words, the Calendar's fixed succession of big themes suggests the smaller themes for single sermons or series of sermons. By following the Calendar, a preacher can at least have *some* idea to start with as he seeks subjects for the Sundays ahead. The important value in using the Church Year for planning purposes is that the Calendar has already taken the first step for you.

The Church Year and the Bible

A WITNESS IN A COURT OF LAW IS ASKED TO SWEAR THAT HE will "tell the truth, the whole truth, and nothing but the truth." If that formula were applied to the pulpit output of most evangelical preachers, the saddest lack would be revealed by the middle one of those three tests. We may insist in all good conscience that we preach the truth and nothing but the truth, but there is a simple way of discovering that many of us fail to preach the *whole* truth. All we have to do is make a list of the books of the Bible and lay along side of it a list of last year's sermon texts. The first time I tried that, I was shocked to learn how little of the whole Scripture, even how little of the whole New Testament, even how little of all the Gospels, I had treated in my preaching. Then I remembered in penitence the charge of the ancient ordinal, some form of which is still used in almost all ordinations, "And be thou a faithful dispenser of the Word of God."

Let a man preach without purpose or plan, and he is likely to ride his hobbies, deal only with his favorite passages of Scripture, and wind up dispensing with the word of God as he more and more becomes merely topical rather than truly textual in his preaching. It may be argued that some portions of Scripture are more edifying than are others. It is surely so that some biblical truths deserve more emphasis than do others. But the final fact is that there is some truth to be found in all of the Bible, in each part of it, and that the whole book has message and meaning for the Church. At least, all of the Bible is worth devout reading and disciplined study, and the point here is that far more of it is worth preaching than commonly receives exposition.

The Church's most ancient insurance that the whole Bible will receive due attention is the use of a lectionary. Writing to preachers in Britain, Russell Clegg, in his article "The Preacher and the Lectionary" published in *The Preacher's Handbook Number 5*, renews the policy in a single sentence: "Those of us who take a 'high' view of the value of Scripture as the authentic word of God must find the case for the use of a lectionary almost unanswerable." Failure to follow some ordered, planned sequence for the reading of the Bible in church services is characterized by the same writer this way:

> Favorite passages are repeatedly heard, but the total amount of Scripture read to the people in a year is pitifully small. The result is that our people are woefully ignorant of the Word of God. Especially is this true of the Old Testament, upon which our understanding of the Teaching of Jesus so greatly depends. Much of our preaching loses in effectiveness because our frequent references to Scripture are not understood. They are not understood because the people are unfamiliar with the passages which we quote. Much as we regret it, we must face

the fact that many of our people do not read their Bibles at home. Dare we continue to leave them in ignorance of the Scriptures? They will remain ignorant so long as we leave the choice of lessons to the individual preacher. Only by the use of a lectionary can we ensure that our people get the wide general acquaintance with Scripture which is needed if they are to be built up in their holy Faith.

From the earliest times lectionaries and calendars have been geared together. If, in turn, preaching is geared to a calendar, there will result a working relationship between the pulpit and the whole Bible. This does not necessarily require that all sermons must have texts selected from the appointed lessons Sunday by Sunday. Neither is it necessary to preach a sermon at some time from every stated lesson. Even the most liturgical communions are not that rigid or mechanical. But what is not enforced by law may well be followed by grace, and it is fairly certain that the preacher who sees the values of a good lectionary for his Sunday services will soon find great values in the lectionary for much of his preaching.

A close relationship between a lectionary and preaching will:

1. ensure broad biblical coverage for the sake of one's people.
2. prevent inappropriateness in observing worth-while special occasions, seasons, and festivals.
3. offer a ready-made, yet sound, source for sermonic materials.
4. prevent the tedium of overemphasis on a few biblical themes.
5. enlarge the range of a preacher's personal study.

6. enhance the variety, color, and interest element of one's whole homiletical product.

Now let's look at the present situation in most of our evangelical American denominations as they are developing a lectionary, particularly as lectionaries are related to the Church Year for Methodists, Presbyterians, Congregationalists, Baptists, and similarly oriented Christians. If I use Methodist materials to illustrate the confusion of the American denominations, it is only because I know my own communion's situation best and because I may be forgiven for criticisms if I level them first at my own church.

Hymnals and service books reveal that most evangelical denominations in America do not provide their preachers and people with an adequate lectionary. Moreover, most evangelical ministers do not understand the traditional principles of a lectionary. However, within the decade of the 1950's, the Methodist Church in Great Britain was developing, revising, and promoting a new lectionary of the Church of England, and doubtless this is influencing Americans more and more. It should be said that English Methodism has always made more use of a lectionary, even the Anglican one, than has American Methodism. In America the Protestant Episcopal Church and the Lutherans are the principal non-Roman users of an official lectionary. Proposals have been made from time to time that a national body like the former Federal Council of Churches or the present National Council of Churches should formulate an agreed-upon lectionary for use in American churches of all denominations. Undoubtedly this will gain headway, for the reading of God's Word by his people in their worship following an ecumenical sequence would offer the same obvious advantages to the search for unity which were long ago discovered in the International Sunday School Lessons, an interdenominational experiment long since widely accepted.

Some attempts to develop a lectionary are already current in American Methodism. In 1935 the *Hymnal* adopted by the Methodist Episcopal Church, the Methodist Episcopal Church, South, and the Methodist Protestant Church contained an Old Testament Lectionary as found on pages 649 and 650 in the current edition. This was adapted to the Church Calendar on page 651 with lessons appointed for special days and observances of the year.

In *The Book of Worship* published by The Methodist Church in 1946, there are two elements of a lectionary. On pages 388 and 389 is a lectionary of epistles and gospels for celebrations of the Holy Communion for the most commonly observed days and seasons of the Church Year. As a member of the commission which prepared *The Book of Worship*, I was assigned the responsibility for arranging this rudimentary eucharistic sequence. Beginning on page 209 in *The Book of Worship* is a calendar and lectionary for the whole of "The Christian Year." I have not made much effort to determine the amount of use these lectionaries enjoy, but I surmise that it is not very extensive.

The Responsive Readings in *The Methodist Hymnal* follow a pattern only vaguely related to the Church Year. This pattern is outlined by the Roman numeral headings of the index. A number of the Church Year observances have Responsive Readings in a special section, and a number of the regular readings have biblical content which is appropriate to Church Year occasions.

Probably the use of an interdenominational lectionary in the common life of free churches will not develop for another generation. Meanwhile, any general practitioner in the parish ministry can find or follow one from some of the sources I shall list in the subsequent pages of this chapter to gain all the attendant values for himself and his people which are listed above. He should, however, understand the traditions of lectionaries.

First, what liturgists call "propers" (Lutherans speak of "pericopes" in the same sense) should be understood. This has to do with the Church Year directly. For each Sunday and for each named occasion of the Calendar there is, for example, a proper psalm. It is contemplated in *The Book of Common Prayer*, moreover, that all of the Psalter will be read day by day within each month, if daily services are held, or within each month if a Christian follows the lectionary in his daily private devotions. This is one of the oldest worship practices of the Hebraic-Christian tradition.

Then for each celebration of the Holy Communion on the Sundays of the Church Year and in observance of its special occasions there are proper epistle and gospel lessons and an accompanying proper collect or prayer. For certain of the most important occasions of the Church Year a Proper Preface precedes the sanctus and follows after the sentence, "It is very meet, right and our bounden duty, . . ." and before the ascription, "Therefore with angels and archangels . . . ." John Wesley kept these Proper Prefaces for the seasons in his abridgment of the Prayer Book, and they may be found by Methodists on page 388 of their *The Book of Worship* or by Presbyterians on page 166 of their *Book of Common Worship*. It is from Proper Prefaces that the liturgists coined the word "propers" for all that marks seasonable observance in worship.

So far, then, as far as a lectionary is concerned, it has been pointed out that there is a psalm for each Sunday and that if Holy Communion is administered on a Sunday, there is an appointed epistle lesson and an appointed gospel lesson. In American Methodist usage the psalm likely would be omitted on a Communion Sunday, but there should be the two readings from the New Testament, one from the epistles and one from the Gospels.

On other than Communion Sundays, the New Testament lesson may properly be *either* from the epistles or the Gospels. It should be said, perhaps, that liturgically *Acts* and *Revelation* are accounted epistles, but on other than Communion Sundays an Old Testament lesson should be read also. In fact, it should come first. Furthermore, a psalm is not regarded as an Old Testament lesson or as a substitute for it according to the ancient lectionary principles. To summarize, the lectionary for Sundays should be like this:

Communion Sundays	*Other Sundays*
An Epistle Lesson	A Psalm
A Gospel Lesson	An Old Testament Lesson
Perhaps a Psalm	Either an Epistle Lesson or A Gospel Lesson

All this poses one of the decisions evangelical Protestants need to make and are even beginning to make. The problem might be stated this way: The same ecclesiastical system which produced the Bible in vernacular language for reading during worship produced the system of propers for the ordered reading of the Bible. The Roman Church first produced a vernacular Bible, the Latin Vulgate; Luther, the German Bible; the Church of England, the King James Version. Why, then, should evangelical Protestants accept gratefully Bibles translated into the language people understand but ignore even the tradition of Lutheranism and Anglicanism which appoints lessons to be read every day, every Sunday, for every occasion? In other words, if the Bible is what we read to our people in our churches, why discard the idea of systematic reading? Furthermore, since there has developed in the long history of Christianity a certain convention or standard called the propers, why not use it? What is gained by being different in our time for the sake of being different from what is of old? By reading an Old Testament lesson and a New Testament lesson at each morning and evening service, the early fathers established a way of reading all or nearly all of the Bible as they worshiped in church. By reading an epistle lesson and a gospel lesson at each Holy Communion, they emphasized that the Sacrament is indeed "blood of the New Testament," as the ancient Prayer of Consecration states it. Is there any better way of emphasizing the New Testament character of the Holy Communion? One after another our major Protestant denominations are moving toward a lectionary of propers.

Much of the confusion about an adequate lectionary at

this stage in contemporary American Methodism grows out of the inclusion of other than psalms in the Responsive Readings in *The Hymnal,* which uses both Old and New Testament material; the failure of *The Hymnal* to match its Old Testament Lectionary (page 649) with a New Testament Lectionary; and the inconsistent mixture of Old Testament and New Testament lessons in the first column of the lectionary for "The Christian Year" on page 209 of *The Book of Worship.* The English Methodists have done far better, I believe. Announcing that "the use of a lectionary is an antidote to the narrowing subjectivity which endangers our Methodist worship," they have established a proper sequence of Bible readings which form a two-year cycle and offer the Old Testament and New Testament in the main during that period.

For the present generation of American Methodists I would suggest that for celebrations of the Holy Communion the propers on pages 388 and 389 of *The Book of Worship* be used as the epistle and gospel lessons; that on other than Communion Sundays the Old Testament lessons be selected over a two-year cycle from pages 649 and 650 of *The Methodist Hymnal;* that the New Testament lessons for other than Communion Sundays be selected on a two-year cycle from pages 209-12 of *The Book of Worship;* and that on other than Communion Sundays the Responsive Reading from *The Hymnal* be the one for any Sunday which happens to be actually a psalm, ignoring completely all Responsive Readings which are not psalms though maybe using their material as one of the lessons. Whether or not a Responsive Reading is a psalm may be determined from the index on pages 645 and 646 in the *Hymnal.* In using the Old Testament Lectionary on pages 649 and 650 in the *Hymnal,* as a two-year cycle, allowance should be made each year for the special observances of the Church Calendar as suggested on page 651. This may prolong the cycle slightly more than two years. Similarly, in developing a two-year cycle of New Testament readings from pages 209-12 in *The Book of Worship,* one should delete the few Old Testament readings from the left column and any references from the right column which correspond to the epistles and gospels used on Communion Sundays from the lectionary on pages 388 and 389. A further word of caution might be added for readers who have had no liturgical conditioning: if you observe there is a difference between the suggested lessons for, say, the First Sunday in Advent as found on page 209 and the suggested lessons for the First Sunday in Advent as found on page 388, remember the latter is intended *only* for use in a Communion Service. If no Communion is planned, use the lessons on page 209. If a Communion is to be celebrated, use the lessons listed on page 388.

By 1946 American Presbyterians had made considerably more progress than Methodists had in 1959 in providing a lectionary for the Church Year, although even in 1959 they did not yet have a complete system of propers. Presbyterians have the advantage also of close affinity with the Church of Scotland, a relationship of which the people themselves in American Presbyterian churches are well aware and more or less value. This means that the minister of an American Presbyterian congregation can make open and acknowledged use of Scottish liturgical materials with probable impunity. Section XI (beginning on page 313) of *Book of Common Order* edited in 1940 by official authorization of the Church of Scotland is entitled

LECTIONARY
Table of Lessons
From Holy Scripture
For Two Years,

and adds under that entitlement, "This lectionary follows the course of the Christian Year. For the Morning Services three Lessons are provided, one from the Old and two from the New Testament, one of the latter being taken from the Gospels." After some information about alternate uses and sources of the table of lessons for evening services, this title page adds, "A Psalm (or Psalms) is also given for each Service."

Here for Presbyterians is the beginning of an adequate system of propers. For a Communion service the two New Testament lessons appointed for the morning service of that Sunday will provide an epistle and gospel. For other than Communion services, an Old Testament and one of the New Testament lessons should be read. And for every Sunday there is a proper from the Psalms. And speaking of the seasonal propers, the Church of Scotland also offers in *The Book of Common Order* proper collects for Communions on Church Year occasions. The 1946 *Book of Common Worship* for American Presbyterians borrowed the Scottish lectionary and other Calendar materials directly. Dr. A. Allan McArthur, of Glasgow, has written an excellent but brief commentary on the Church of Scotland's rediscovery of its lectionary under the title *The Christian Year and Lectionary Reform* (London: SCM Press, 1958) and offers an alternative system of lessons which he calls the Peterhead Lectionary. An American Presbyterian, or for that matter any evangelical churchman, would do well to study McArthur's suggestions. The 1955 edition of *The Hymnbook*, in official use among most Presbyterians, however, does the same thing *The Methodist Hymnal* does in departing from the Psalms for responsive readings, and includes selections from both the prophets and the New Testament. Some readings in the Presbyterian hymnbook are for unison rather than responsive use, a novel notion. There is a table on page 467 suggesting readings thought to be appropriate for a number of Christian Year occasions. But aside from these readings, *The Hymnbook* offers no directions about morning and evening lessons from the Old and New Testaments nor epistles and gospels for Communion services.

In an earlier edition of *The Book of Common Worship* for American Presbyterians, the Psalter, meaning Psalms only, was slightly abridged and appended to this book. At the beginning of this Psalter was a brief listing which began, "The following Selections may be read as appropriate for certain days," and the Calendar occasions mentioned are just these few: Good Friday, Easter Day, Advent, and Christmas Day. However, several psalms are suggested for each of these times; so it might be well worth comparing this little table with the one in *The Hymnal* mentioned in the previous paragraph. It should be noted here in passing that *The Book of Common Worship* (1946) in its section "The Treasury of Prayers" has a subsection containing a number of prayers for "Certain Times and Seasons," including various Calendar occasions. These may serve as proper collects.

Congregationalists (even those in America now merged with the Evangelical and Reformed Church) and Presbyterians (or Methodists, too, for that matter) might feel enough kinship with the United Church of Canada to welcome some help in the formation of a proper lectionary from the Canadian *Book of Common Order*, for it will be remembered that the United Church of Canada originally united Congregationalists, Presbyterians, and Methodists. *The Book of Common Order* of the United Church of Canada is one of the finest bridges in ecumenical Christianity between liturgical traditionalism and evangelical practice. A whole chapter is entitled "A Table of Lessons" and is organized on the basis of the Church Year. Incidentally, brief italicized headings for each liturgical season are among the best descriptions I know of the significance of the days and occasions of the Calendar. For each Sunday a proper collect is printed, presumably for use in Communion services, and generally three lessons, one from the Old Testament, an epistle, and a gospel, are suggested. Unfortunately this is not the case for every Sunday, so some difficulty will arise in trying to find a proper for every Sunday. Sometimes an Old Testament lesson is not listed, which will make lectionary problems for Sunday when there is to be no Communion service, and sometimes there is not listed for a particular Sunday both an epistle and a gospel, which does not adequately provide for the possibility of a Communion service on any Sunday of the year. Nevertheless, considerable progress toward a full and complete system of propers, both lessons and prayers, is evident in the Canadian book.

A number of former Congregational churches and even more Baptist churches use *The American Hymnal,* I am told. This publication has no specific denominational label, however. It contains a section of responsive readings, though not all are psalms. Several selections are listed as suitable for Christmas, Lent, Good Friday, and Easter, which is at least a rudimentary relationship between the Bible and the Calendar. This is about the same in *Pilgrim Hymnal* used by many Congregationalists. A hymnbook entitled *Christian Worship* published by the Baptist Judson Press begins with a section of responsive readings introduced with this comment, "The Readings from both the Old and the New Testaments have been provided for each Sunday to meet the need of pastors who desire to use two Scripture lessons in the same service." There is also an index for these readings suggesting suitable ones for such Calendar topics as "Advent of Jesus," All Saints, Easter, Pentecost (Whitsunday), and so forth. The American Baptist Publication Society's *New Baptist Hymnal* concludes with a number of responsive readings from both the Old and New Testaments, but the only Calendar day mentioned by name in the topical listing of these readings is, interestingly enough, Palm Sunday. The recent merger of the Congregational Christian denomination with the Evangelical and Reformed Church will offer to the former the latter's *Book of Worship* (1943) containing a section entitled "The Church Year" and listing such propers as introits, collects, epistles, gospels, and Old and New Testament lessons in a very complete form which is also published in the 1941 edition of *The*

Hymnal of the Evangelical and Reformed Church. Congregationalists will find this a very great gain indeed.

Two manuals much used by Free Church clergy, especially by Baptists, Disciples, and Congregationalists, I believe, are a *Book of Common Worship* compiled in 1932 by Wilbur P. Thirkield and Oliver Huckel, and *Minister's Service Book* edited in 1937 by James Dalton Morrison with a commendation by Albert W. Beaven as president of Colgate-Rochester Divinity School. The former makes considerable reference to the Church Year in arranging its materials, prayers, aids to worship, and so forth, and contains a section entitled "The Psalter and Other Responsive Readings from the Holy Scripture." This in turn is introduced by a table making suggestions "For Special Subjects, Days, or Seasons" which contains such Calendar listings as Advent, Christmas, Lent, Palm Sunday, Holy Week, Good Friday, Easter, Ascension Day, Pentecost, and All Saints' with more than one reading opposite these. While *Minister's Service Book* offers neither responsive readings nor a full-fledged lectionary, it might be possible for a minister to expand some of the scriptural calls to worship and other sentences arranged under various Calendar and other headings into longer lessons.

The evangelical minister whose denomination does not provide a complete lectionary or at least not complete propers for the Church Year may find himself turning to one of three sources for ready-made listings. The Protestant Episcopal *Book of Common Prayer* contains a lectionary of Old Testament and New Testament lessons for morning and evening services and an organization of psalms for the entire year. For Holy Communion there are propers for all Sundays and Calendar occasions consisting of a collect, an epistle lesson, and a gospel lesson; and for Holy Communion on certain principal occasions there is a Proper Preface to the Sanctus. The new Lutheran *Common Service Book* which is combined with a hymnal offers alternative pericopes of Old Testament, epistle, and gospel lessons and propers of the Church Year as to introits from Scripture, Psalms, graduals, and collects.[1] If using Episcopalian or Lutheran sources makes a Free Church minister feel too imitative, he will be extremely fortunate if he can find the little pamphlet now out of print entitled *The Christian Year* which was edited by Fred Winslow Adams for the Committee on Worship of the former Federal Council of Churches of Christ in America. It appeared first in 1937 and again in 1940 and contains a complete lectionary.

Of course, it is possible, though it is very hard work, to outline a biblical year for oneself. Still more possible, considering the individualism as preachers which all of us share, is the selection of suitable Old Testament and New Testament lessons for our own preaching purposes on certain occasions. A *Nave's Topical Bible* and *The New Topical Text Book*, published in 1935 by Fleming H. Revell Company will prove major aids. There will always come times when for reasons acceptable at least to himself, any preacher will need and want to select as lessons portions of the Scripture not listed in any formal lectionary of sequence. To do this well requires us to live with our Bibles

[1] In two volumes published by Concordia Publishing House in 1958, Fred H. Lindemann offers detailed sermon material for Calendar occasions based on the Lutheran pericope propers. He calls them *The Sermon and the Propers*, and Volume I is for Advent and Epiphany, while Volume II is for Pre-Lent to Pentecost.

constantly and to know the Scriptures by thorough study.

A minister needs to read his Bible at least two ways: personally and devotionally as a Christian, and studiously and homiletically as a preacher. From the first there will come frequent inspirations he will not hesitate to use in the pulpit; from the second he will be refreshed again and again spiritually and individually. There is, then, an overlapping of the two approaches, and this is good. Nevertheless, it is possible to make a plan for each.

For purposes of serious study and preaching it has been my practice to use the following sequence in order to ensure for my people a general treatment of the whole Bible each four years. This means the purchasing of new books as they may appear since the last rotation, and the reviewing of old notes and previously prepared materials, as well as the development of new sermons or teaching courses.

Where I have had regular Sunday evening services, I have usually preached a series of sermons every year from such groupings of Bible books as the so-called minor prophets or the General epistles or the Pastoral epistles. Sometimes I have preached a short one-month series from single books such as Genesis or the Revelation.

Following the Church Year Calendar it is possible to relate one's preaching to some such sequence as this which follows. It should be remembered, of course, that texts and materials from any or all biblical books may be used any one year intermingled with materials from the books of the four-year plan. This is more a guide for a preacher's own study than for anything else, but it does produce values for one's people. Some biblical books are repeated within two years instead of four, both because of their importance and because of their length.

FIRST YEAR

Genesis, Exodus	Matthew
Joshua, Judges	Romans
Ruth	Timothy, Titus, Philemon
Psalms	Corinthians
Isaiah	
Ezekiel	

SECOND YEAR

Deuteronomy	Mark
Samuel	Hebrews
Ezra	Galatians
Job	Ephesians
Jeremiah	Philippians
Daniel	Colossians

THIRD YEAR

Leviticus, Numbers	Luke, the Acts
Kings	Revelation
Nehemiah	Thessalonians
Isaiah	Romans
The Minor Prophets, First Six	

FOURTH YEAR

Deuteronomy	John
Chronicles	Hebrews
Esther	James, Peter, John
Ecclesiastes, Song of Solomon, Lamentations	

Jeremiah
The Minor Prophets, Second Six

But lectionaries are not meant to be mechanical, nor need they restrict in any formal, merely liturgical way, the free flow of God's word in his Church. Like all things in the Church humanly devised, they serve only as vehicles for grace. In the Standard Sermon on "The Means of Grace," John Wesley defined them as Prayer, Searching the Scripture, and the Lord's Supper. Preaching must search the Scripture better than it does in most evangelical pulpits today, and search with a wider range, a more inclusive scope, and a more carefully planned purpose if we are to be "faithful dispensers of the Word of God" in our age.

The Calendar in Music

BECAUSE I AM SO CONVINCED THAT AN APPRECIATION AND application of the Church Year Calendar will never come fully into the life of evangelical Protestantism unless and until it comes into the pulpit, most of this book is about preaching. However we remodel our chancels, the pulpit remains central in the cultus of the Free Churches.

But if preaching is paramount among us, we, nevertheless, attach considerable importance to other components of our worship as well. One of our freedoms is the perfect right to draw upon the devotions of Christian people of every era and every persuasion. This catholicity is nowhere better demonstrated among evangelicals than in our denominational hymnals, yet such manuals as Methodism's *Book of Worship* and Presbyterianism's *Book of Common Worship* also illustrate modern Protestantism's willingness to use worship materials from almost every ancient and contemporary source.

Certain stages of development are observable. For example, there is a decade's progress in churchmanship to be seen by comparing the 1935 edition of *The Methodist*

Hymnal with Methodism's *Book of Worship.* The former had a section entitled "Aids to Individual and Congregational Devotion" at first only for use in the Methodist Episcopal Church but which was not contained in printings for the Methodist Episcopal Church, South or Methodist Protestant Church. By 1940 *The Hymnal* was printed with this material for use throughout the united Church, and in 1946 this general material was expanded to include additional Calendar materials in *The Book of Worship,* such as versicles and collects for the seasons of the Christian Year. Somewhat the same progression as to both the amount of liturgical material and the degree of conformity to the Calendar may be noted in the 1946 Presbyterian *Book of Common Worship* as contrasted with its predecessor, although this is not as clear when contrasting the 1955 *The Hymnbook* with *The Presbyterian Hymnal* prior to that year. From a liturgical and calendar viewpoint it seems to me that Presbyterians in America have gained more in their prayer book than in their hymnal. Anyhow, more and more of Christian devotion is being made available to all our evangelical denominations, and increasingly the Calendar is being used as a worthy and pragmatic way of organizing these materials for use in worship. However, as things stand now, we are still under the necessity of digging out Church Year materials from our hymnals because there has not yet appeared much classification of them in Calendar categories.

But it is to hymns that we must mostly look now to adapt the worship services of our evangelical churches to the Calendar. Fortunately, all denominations acknowledge the great English hymn writer who produced the largest volume of hymns by a single author, Charles Wesley, who, as an Anglican if not as a Methodist, took the Calendar seriously and wrote many hymns for seasonal yet evangelical use. Of course, other hymn writers have done this also. There are some hymns, therefore, in all our Protestant hymnbooks which relate to Church Year occasions even if they are not arranged to conform to the Calendar.

Even Charles Wesley did not always designate his hymns by the Calendar, so let me use one of his best-known hymns which is in nearly every denominational hymnal to illustrate how evangelical ministers will need to "dig out" from their hymnals appropriate Calendar music. Look at this stanza:

> Love divine, all loves excelling,
> Joy of heaven, to earth come down;
> Fix in us Thy humble dwelling,
> All Thy faithful mercies crown!
> Jesus, Thou art all compassion,
> Pure, unbounded love Thou art;
> Visit us with Thy salvation,
> Enter every trembling heart.

Isn't this an almost perfect treatment of the Incarnation? Use it for Christmastide. Now look at two other stanzas of the same hymn:

> Come, Almighty to deliver,
> Let us all Thy grace receive;
> Suddenly return, and never,
> Never more Thy temples leave.
> Thee we would be always blessing,

Serve Thee as Thy hosts above,
Pray, and praise Thee without ceasing,
Glory in Thy perfect love.

Finish, then, Thy new creation;
Pure and spotless let us be;
Let us see Thy great salvation
Perfectly restored in Thee:
Changed from glory into glory,
Till in heaven we take our place,
Till we cast our crowns before Thee,
Lost in wonder, love, and praise.

Surely here is the Advent message at its finest. How would it do then to let such a hymn as this in its entirety bridge that difficult transition Sunday, the fourth in December, between Advent and Christmastide. It is one of our problem Sundays since so many evangelical congregations find it hard not to observe Christmas on the Sunday before Christmas Day when they should be still observing Advent.

Although they may not be classified in your denominational hymnal as Advent hymns, here are two more you might "dig out" for Advent use: "Lift up your heads, ye mighty gates," which is usually thought of as a Palm Sunday hymn, and "Watchman, tell us of the night," which might possibly serve also as an Epiphany hymn. As I suggested in the case of "Love Divine, all loves excelling," so I am trying to illustrate again with these two hymns that gold is for the digging, and that ministers may well mine their own seasonal music out of many more parts of their hymnals than may already have Calendar headings provided by the editors or publishers.

Actually, Advent and Epiphany are the two Calendar seasons when the number of hymns available in most hymnals of American Protestant denominations is limited and when there is difficulty avoiding confusion with Christmas. Most hymnals contain these classic Advent hymns:

"Come, Thou long expected Jesus, . . . "
"O come, O come, Immanuel, . . ."
"Hail, to the Lord's anointed, . . . "

Other slightly less known but excellent Advent hymns are:

"Comfort ye, comfort ye my people,"
"The King shall come when morning dawns,"

which may be found in several hymnals including the 1940 edition of *The Hymnal* of the Protestant Episcopal Church or the 1941 edition of *The Hymnal* of the Evangelical and Reformed Church, the two books which best classify hymns according to the Calendar. Here are Advent hymns which are in several denominational hymnals, including these two, which might be printed in a Sunday's worship folder if they are not contained in your own denominational book. I am listing these because they may be set respectively to some tune familiar to your own people:

"Hark! the glad sound! the Saviour comes, . . ."
"Arise, the kingdom is at hand, . . ."
"The Lord is come, on Syrian soil, . . ."

An excellent Advent hymn, which I mention because good Advent hymns are so hard to find in sufficient number in most denominational hymnals, is in the Presbyterians' new *Hymnbook* and may be set to any familiar C. M. tune. It is "The race that long in darkness pined," and it expresses true Advent meaning.

If it is used toward the end of Advent, "Joy to the world! the Lord is come" may not be inappropriate. It does lift up the great hopes of Advent, and its line "Let every heart prepare Him room" certainly strikes an authentic Advent note. Perhaps the biggest problem in selecting hymns for the Advent services is how to resist popular pressure to sing Christmas hymns and carols. Most of us will probably have to compromise about this at least on the Sunday before Christmas Day. Two Christmas hymns which deserve greater use are Tillett's "O Son of God incarnate" and Farrington's "I know not how that Bethlehem's Babe could in the Godhead be." Both are relatively modern and both contain in fine verses the doctrine of the Incarnation, which, of course, is what Christmas is all about.

The Christmas hymns are too well known to need treatment here. The well-known hymns, "As with gladness men of old did the guiding star behold" and "We three kings of Orient are" are Epiphany, not Christmas, hymns. Most of our people keep pulling the Wise Men much too soon into their celebration of Christ's nativity. By the time Epiphany comes, they wonder why preachers are still talking about the Magi when clearly Christmas is past! It's too bad, but the cure will take time—at least as long a time as it takes to get a new hymnal edition in several denominations.

For Epiphany, in addition to the two mentioned, there

are such fine hymns as Wesley's "Christ, whose glory fills the skies," Heber's classic "Brightest and best of the sons of the morning," "We would see Jesus; lo! His star is shining," "Light of the world, we hail Thee," and such standard missionary hymns as "O Zion, haste, thy mission, high fulfilling, to tell to all the world that God is Light" and "From all the dark places Of earth's heathen races, O see how the thick shadows fly." Some relatively modern hymns with excellent Epiphany values are Samuel F. Smith's "The morning light is breaking," Hasting's "Hail to the brightness of Zion's glad morning," Tweedy's "Eternal God, whose power upholds both flower and flaming star," Burton's "There's a light upon the mountains," and Ozora Davis' "At length there dawns the glorious day By prophets long foretold."

A good Epiphany hymn set to some C. M. D. tune which might be printed in a worship leaflet is from *The Hymnbook* of the Presbyterian Church, "O sing a song of Bethlehem." This is not a Christmas hymn even if its opening words make it sound like a carol. A favorite of all Epiphany hymns, however, must surely be the familiar tune *Righini* sung with Marriott's stanzas, the first of which begins "Thou, whose almighty word Chaos and darkness heard," and each stanza of which ends with the great Epiphany exclamation, "Let there be light!"

The hymns one selects for congregational use in Lent may be as varied as are the preaching themes one prepares, for Lent need not have a single subject content. Naturally there will be an emphasis on our Lord's passion, at least near the end of Lent and in Holy Week. Every Protestant hymnbook contains hymns in abundance for this period.

What we most need to learn in our worship each spring is to sing hymns of the Resurrection after Easter Sunday itself. Just as too many Protestants cut off their celebration of Christ's nativity too soon and fail to carry it through to its climax in Epiphany, so we have all too often stopped Eastertide at its very start, observing only Easter Sunday. Some of our modern hymn writers, especially, have given us hymns for use through the whole of Eastertide. Let me mention only Masefield's "Sing, men and angels, sing" and Shillito's "Away with gloom, away with doubt!"

For the celebration of the Ascension, Wesley's "Ye servants of God, your Master proclaim" like many other hymns about the everliving Christ is also an excellent choice for Kingdomtide. More specifically, Ascension hymns, however, would include "The Head that once was crowned with thorns," "Look, ye saints! The sight is glorious," "Hail, Thou once despised Jesus!," "Hark! ten thousand harps and voices," and "Crown Him with many crowns, The Lamb upon His throne."

Hymns about the Church and about the Holy Spirit will naturally be chosen for Whitsunday. A modern hymn by Tweedy, "O Spirit of the Living God, Thou Light and Fire Divine: descend upon Thy Church one more and make it truly Thine!" combines the two themes better than any I know for an observance of the Pentecost.

The hymn of hymns for Trinity Sunday is naturally "Holy, holy, holy," which should not be worn out as an opening hymn at Holy Communion repeatedly. Of course, there is "Come, Thou almighty King" as an alternative for Trinity Sunday. Or again, *Righini* may be used on Trinity Sunday as well as for Epiphany.

In the long sequence of Sundays "after Trinity" and in Kingdomtide, only one Calendar occasion may require its own hymnody—All Saints'. Wesley's best for this observance is "Come, let us join our friends above." The two most familiar hymns in this category, however, are probably "For all the saints, who from their labors rest" and "Ten thousand times ten thousand in sparkling raiment bright."

In concluding this chapter, perhaps we should give some attention to responses, introits, vespers, and the like. The singing of such sentences and versicles has come to be a common feature in evangelical Protestant services although recent liturgical purists are decrying these "petty prettifications." The well-known lines of "Let all mortal flesh keep silence" are most appropriate for Christmas but possibly might serve as an Advent introit as well. There is a brief chant of "Glory to God in the highest, and on earth peace to men in whom He is well pleased," which is in several hymnbooks and which will be useful in Christmas services. It should be remembered that the *Gloria Patri* is not usually chanted in Advent and Lent, because the psalms for those seasons are penitential rather than acts of praise.

The words "Through love to light!" have been set to the familiar tune *Finlandia* and have Epiphany meanings as does also the chant "Hail, gladdening Light."

In Eastertide one might wish to use the introit which has become more and more common in Protestantism, "Jesus, stand among us in Thy risen power" and also the benediction, "Now may He who from the dead brought the Shepherd of the sheep."

An Ascension line which has music by Mendelssohn-

Bartholdy is "Hear Thou in love, O Lord, our cry, in heaven, Thy dwelling place on high."

If musical amens must be used, perhaps there is justification for a sevenfold amen on Whitsunday and a threefold amen on Trinity Sunday. May I say, however, that when evangelical clergy begin what has been called "adorning" and "enriching" their services without good judgment and reason for what they do, they do much to defeat the wholesome development of liturgical appreciation.

Out of Personal Experience

ONE MAY NOT HONESTLY SEND A STRANGER ON A ROUTE ONE has traveled without warning against any known dangers. A national automobile club always marks the detours and construction, the sections of rough road, and the washed-out bridges on any map it gives it members, and this is important service. Similarly, in commending the Church Year to fellow evangelicals, it is only honest, and I trust important, too, for me to describe some of the dangers I have experienced myself in working with the Calendar.

An evangelical should be under constant conviction that the gospel itself is not controlled by seasons. Jesus Christ is the same yesterday and today and forever. In other words, the Calendar does not make the Christian message; exactly the opposite is the truth. The danger I have confronted in using the Church Year in preaching is the temptation to ask, "What will make a good sermon for Epiphany?" rather than, "What gospel does the Epiphany prompt me to preach?" It is not the evangelical's business to preach the Church Calendar, but to preach the gospel of Christ, so evangelicals should be on guard against preaching Advent sermons or Christmas sermons or Epiphany sermons or Lenten sermons or any such seasonal sermons. They are called to preach the gospel in Advent, at Christmas, of the Epiphany, during Lent, yes, in season and out of season, everywhere and all the time.

But the Calendar has helped me avoid some of the individualism which plagues the Protestant pulpit. Evangelical Protestantism's fascination with preaching, despite all the concomitant values of that, has tempted us to build churches around preachers and has tempted many a preacher to become a prima donna. The Church Year may help a preacher be creative, inventive, and imaginative, but the Calendar with its great themes marks out a map of the gospel beyond which there is little place for a preacher's own bizarre notions. Again and again it will pull him back on course when he begins to confuse his own opinions with the gospel.

For it must be remembered that the Church produced the Bible, rather than that the Bible produced the Church. Then the Church produced the Calendar to teach that Bible. It is the Church's historic "course of study."

The Church Year as a program for preaching has kept me studying. The very element of repetition which a Calendar embraces is itself a prod, prompting one to treat freshly and effectively each year's recurring occasions. For the truth which every general practitioner of the parish ministry will confess is that habits of study are hard to hold under the pressures of pastoral and administrative responsibilities. Without some organized approach to study a pastor is likely to dabble around in his reading, depending far too much on digests and reviews. Although I am as ashamed as the next man of books unread and study skimped, I am at least certain that I have done far more solid studying than I would have done without some such practical guide as the Church Year. At least, it has given me some criterion for buying books, some idea of what to look for, and some plan for laying out my reading for the hours I can snatch out of every busy day.

Moreover, I have witnessed the contributions the Church Year has made to my people. This is the most important consideration of all. Plain people need pegs on which to hang their spiritual experiences and their religious understandings. Like all good things, this need has inherent dangers, but the need itself is not necessarily bad. Mere mechanics may be substituted for real experience, and this is the old, standard argument of the Puritans against churchmanship. But without mechanics emotions may be substituted for motion; that is, there may be no effective harnessing of the spiritual power of preaching and worship to the lives of people. It is true that the instincts of an evangelical must guard and govern against deadly ritualism and sterile formalism. But the most avowed evangelical can find at least some values in such ancient observances as the Church Year. If the observance of Christmas, for example, has persisted despite all Puritan attempts to label it popery, why not accept the the observance of other Calendar occasions? Actually, evangelical Protestantism has been as busy making special occasions—Rally Day, Children's Day, Temperance Sunday, Mother's Day, to name a few—as ever was the most medieval hagiographer.

Of course, it may be a matter of opinion, but I think I have observed real evidence of how some of the traditions of churchmanship have helped my people be and become better Christians. Once again, I must insist that no loss of the evangelical spirit has been suffered. It has been greatly gratifying to witness how much more knowledgeable and intelligent about their faith many of my congregation have become after some years of *thinking* theology organized around an easily followed plan. Expressions of appreciation have been numerous, such as, "At last, I'm beginning to get the whole picture," or, "It's all beginning to add up," or similar comments indicating that people are helped when there is a clearly discernible pattern to preaching and worship.

A temptation which is more likely to beset young preachers, I think, is the danger of letting the Calendar become a toy. This is especially a danger to the preacher who has just discovered the liturgical pattern. He will be tempted to play with it, to juggle with it. To put this another way, he may become romantic about the liturgical implications of the Calendar. After all, the Free Churches of America have had comparatively little experience with liturgical matters in recent generations, and it is natural that such things as seasonal colors, particularly for paraments (colored chancel draperies) and stoles, or seasonal prayers and lessons should now somewhat intrigue modern churchmen. There is always an excitement about what is novel.

The shield against this complex of temptation is to regard the Calendar always as a means and never as an end. It is a useful and worthy vehicle, but only that. It is not the whole gospel, but it helps ensure the proclamation of the whole gospel. It is not a hobby, but helps preachers avoid hobby riding. Its appurtenances are wholly incidental and secondary, for the eternal message of salvation must be proclaimed every Sunday and every season regardless, for example, of what color ornaments the pulpit. The progression of priority goes like this: colors may help people follow the sequence of the Calendar, and the Calendar does help people follow the sequence of those mighty acts of God which reveal his grace, and that grace proclaimed always helps people find and accept Christ.

Speaking of seasonal colors, may I suggest that the ancient Sarum sequence might be more appropriate in Protestant usage than is the better-known Roman system of white, red, violet, green and black. I must confess that I have not yet been able to introduce this in a church which I have served myself, because I have either found paraments for pulpit, lectern, and altar already provided or did not know the Sarum use in my earlier ministry; but if I were to serve now a new church or one which did not possess such antependia already, I think I would like to secure only the red, white, and blue sets rather than use the five colors of the Roman tradition. This is not just American patriotism on my part, believe me, though I have appreciated that what the Episcopalians call the "National" Cathedral in Washington, D.C., has followed the Sarum use with patriotic appropriateness in our capital city. Let me first explain that in the old English tradition which centered around Salisbury Cathedral, blue and violet were regarded as the same color, as perhaps they were by all ancients. Thus, white would be the color of innocency and festivity for use on the great occasions of our Lord's nativity, resurrection, and ascension; blue, the penitential or solemn color, would be used for Advent and Lent; and red, the color of fire, signifying the militancy of the Church inspired by the Holy Spirit, would be used for all other occasions and seasons. This seems to me to be a simpler and more straightforward system of symbolism than the Roman one which introduces the muddy ecclesiastical green of nature for ferial times and leaves Protestants little use for red except on Whitsunday, since we do not observe saints' days. Red has come to be used in some places when Kingdomtide is observed, but I doubt if this is general though I think it is very good.

It is possible to become too schematic. I think this may be all the more tempting the more logical and orderly one's temperament may be, though surely it must be a temptation to quick and clever homilecticians as well. Sermon series have great value, for they permit larger or deeper treatment of truth than do single sermons. Yet, seasonal series might turn out to be very weak or thin if they are devised only to extend a single theme through several Sundays. A preacher who has three good and sound sermons for Advent may find that the Calendar tempts him to add a clever but shallow discourse just to fill out the four-Sundays-in-Advent scheme, for example. His sense of order prompts him to want four instead of just three observances of Advent for no better reason than that there are four Advent Sundays in the Calendar. What may be worse is that he might be tempted to discard his three good sermons, which would help his people, only because he can't relate a fourth sermon to the first three.

James A. Pike, in a foreword which introduces a compendium entitled *Preaching the Christian Year* begins by saying:

> The traditional Christian Year is the Church's safeguard against the idiosyncrasies of its ministers. By spreading the "mighty acts of God" over a span of time each year, it encourages—though it does not guarantee—a balanced diet for the spiritual nurture of the laymen, and it challenges the preacher to encompass all of the essential elements of the Christian message.[1]

This is the protection the Calendar offers against its own temptations. Then he adds, "But the Christian Year does not limit the freedom of the preacher. It does not put words in his mouth." As he says there is protection but not guarantee. Freedom has its inevitable risks.

Sooner or later American evangelicals must come to terms with what is being called the liturgical movement. Only then shall we be cured from unreasonable suspicions on the one hand and slavish imitations on the other. A hundred years have elapsed since the time of the Tractarians who sought the recovery of catholic faith and order for the heirs of the Reformation. Their basic concern has grown in influence ever since. However new it may seem to today's churchmen of the more separatist or independent tradition, the liturgical movement is not actually a new fad or a sudden fashion. It has been gaining ground for a long time, and it is here to stay for a long time in the life of nearly all denominations.

The word "catholic" usually connotes universality and historicity, if one may ignore the ignorance of those to whom it connotes only popery. What it might well come to mean, however, is "standard." The recovery of our catholic faith and order will mean the erection of time-

[1] Published by Charles Scribner's Sons.

tested and widely accepted standards of truth and usage within the Reformed Church, standards to which all may repair gladly and freely. It was the loss of these standards during the cultural lag of frontier times in America which produced some of the extremes of individualism, some of the bizarre practices, and some of the multiplication of splinter sects. A failure to define adequately and accept intelligently catholic standards may mean continued faddishness and exotic ritualism. We need standards which unify the Christian witness without compelling picayune uniformity. The Calendar is just such a standard.

Strange how evangelical Protestants have feared churchmanship! The Puritan Separatists left us a great heritage, but the inheritance tax was exorbitant. At times we have even made a virtue of crudeness or a cult of ugliness in our fear of all that would add color and drama to our worship. Two decades of as much liturgical experience as following the Church Year affords makes me feel sure that the Calendar is a sound vehicle for evangelism and that it supports what has long been my evangelical idea: a warmly persuasive sermon in the setting of finely ordered worship.

A Christian of the Reformed tradition knows that Christianity staggered up out of the Dark Ages with the impedimenta of pagan superstition on its back. The Protestant Revolution, for that's what it was, stripped the overlay as much as possible in its laudable zeal to reach the bare and beautiful grain of that apostolic truth of which Christ's Church is essentially constructed. That is mixing figures, I know, but what I mean is that in shucking off the baggage of superstition our fathers may have left lying on the ground some of the Church's most valuable possessions, or to mix some more figures, in scraping off the paint of paganism, they may have scarred and scratched the beauty of the Church's life. Maybe all that is just a fancy way of saying that evangelical Protestantism went too far once the Reformation Revolution got going.

But for evangelicals the ultimate test will never be made solely in terms of more thoughtful theology or more definite discipline; they will always ask whether something helps or hinders the winning of disciples and the deepening of devotion. Now as to the first aspects of that, it must be said that there is a cultural problem to deal with. As a matter of fact, I often wonder whether the real distinction today between "liturgical" and "evangelical" isn't as much a cultural as a theological one. Therefore, the use of the Church Year in Free Church worship will require education and promotion before it becomes effective. As the general educational level in America arises, this is becoming true about many other aspects of church life as well. Frontier and primitive conditions no longer obtain, and it is almost demagoguery to try to keep evangelical Protestants oriented to frontier folkways. However, we must start with people as we find them. Often we find them with an ingrained suspicion of anything which even remotely seems or sounds Roman Catholic.

So the first step in introducing the Church Year probably will be to point out that it has denominational approval and general acceptance. Methodists can be shown that the Church Year is actually printed in the denomination's official hymnal (page 651). Another well-worked device for helping Methodists accept various churchly practices and viewpoints is to quote John Wesley: such as his commendation of his Sunday Service as an abridgment of Anglican liturgy. Presbyterians can find similar support from Scottish sources or point to Calvin's general directory for worship, and doubtless other denominations can find enough in their history to establish the truth that churchmanship does not necessarily suggest Roman Catholicism.

But if this first step is negative or apologetic, the positive values inherent in the Church Year must be taught with conviction and patience. Choirs are good groups with which to begin, and youth groups are also. A pastor should enlist the support of his church-school faculty and his lay officials early in the teaching process. After a while the Calendar will commend itself. Then it will begin to offer the kind of definiteness and clarity which is its most vital character. This in turn will become an effective tool to convince and convert, because Church Year preaching has point and pith to it and helps a preacher avoid the vague generalities which seldom win disciples. If the Church Year helps a preacher keep to a given subject at a given time, it offers specific challenge to his hearers. Instead of general sermons on "Come to Jesus," Church Year preaching in Advent invites hearers to "Come to the Jesus who came, is here, and is coming again"; in Epiphany, "Come, help Jesus shine in a dark world"; and in Lent, "Come to the Jesus who was tempted, tried, killed, and who can pull you out of the same death." I know such preaching "works" when somebody says, "I can grab hold of what you're talking about," or, "I can get my teeth into that now." That ought to be the reaction and response to all evangelical preaching. The Church Year helps get that.

It also helps develop devotion. People need leading in

learning to pray and praise. The Church Year is a chart and compass in this respect also. Lessons, hymns, anthems, and responses may all be more readily and yet more effectively selected if the Calendar is the frame of reference for the minister preparing a worship service. Just as good series preaching helps people feel the importance of a Church Year season so that they will be especially attentive, so the use of a single bulletin or order of worship for all the Sundays of each such season as Advent, Epiphanytide, and Lent will help people focus their devotions throughout a whole period. This will deepen habits of worship and fix patterns of spirituality.

In introducing this book I promised that I would deal only with the "possibles," with what can be assimilated now in evangelical denominations without creating serious problems. However, I would like to think that possibilities change and grow, so let me at least mention some Calendar days which may be observed in our Free Churches sometime in the future. Frankly, I have never made use of these occasions myself, but that is no proof that I never shall. I offer them here as "some days for someday, maybe":

First, there is a group of saints' days:
St. Andrew's, November 30
St. Thomas', December 21
St. Stephen's, December 26
St. John's, December 27
The Conversion of St. Paul, January 25

just to list those which come within the winter season. Now, I doubt if evangelical churches are ever going to do much with most of these. For one thing, they come on week days rather than Sundays usually, or if on Sundays, then are properly superseded by observances of Advent, Christmastide, and Epiphanytide. However, when a saint's day and a Sunday did coincide, I think I might find something I wanted to say about a hero of our heritage. In other words, I don't think we need to be afraid to mention a saint or even to give one that title. The day connected with one of the New Testament worthies which might prove very useful indeed for making a thoroughly evangelical witness is the Conversion of Paul. Surely we can point out with penetrating truth that when a Saul becomes a Paul, he is on the way to sainthood; that when men gain a new nature in Christ, they may gain both a new name and a new title. I believe the Protestant Reformation cured any likelihood that we shall ever let hagiography become a problem for us. I think we ought to relax about the saints, take them or leave them, but not fear them. Yet maybe the best thing we can do about saints at this stage of our Protestant development is to show the very real identity between Reformation Day and All Saints' Day and how all Christians should aspire to be saints, in honor preferring one another who have achieved that sainthood.

Holy Innocents' Day is December 28. Somewhere in the touching tragedy of their story must lie a great message about the kind of sin our own generation has witnessed in the atrocities of two world wars and about the judgment which hangs over our age. But I'm reasonably sure that if Christmas Sunday should come on that date, the Holy Innocents of Bethlehem would yield in our devotions to the innocent Babe for whom they died. Maybe some better preacher than I will find a way to tell their story in the name of that Babe, so I mention them here as the least I can do.

On what the secular world calls New Year's Day, the Church has for many, many years remembered the circumcision and naming of Jesus. The Presentation of Jesus and the Purification of Mary in the Temple is observed on February 2. A message on Holy Baptism, or on the devotion of a Christian dedication might be proclaimed helpfully and appropriately on either the January 1 or February 2 occasion. Incidentally, the February 2 date is sometimes called "Candlemas." Some churches use it for an Epiphany service called a Festival of Lights.

Lutherans observe the Transfiguration of Jesus on the last Sunday in Epiphanytide. There is inspired and inspiring preaching in the account of Christ's great experience of transfiguration which no Protestant will hesitate to offer.

I'm not sure that Protestants will find themselves observing the Annunciation to Mary on March 25, however; almost certainly it will be crowded out by other Lenten considerations or by our suspicion of Mariolatry in general.

If these or any other of the lesser festivals appeal to you and you desire some sermonic guidance, the best I can suggest is in the two volumes of Fred H. Lindemann's *The Sermon and the Propers*, published in 1958 by Concordia Publishing House, St. Louis. Although writing from a very Lutheran viewpoint, Lindemann does provide textual and other source materials for all these days.

Well, to summarize it all, the argument for using the Church Year is the argument for system versus clutter, order versus disorder, and plan versus procrastination. I shall be sad if it all sounds pedantic, too precise and contrived.

To me, at least, the Church Year has brought both faith and the freedom to proclaim it, has never stifled inspiration, nor held me knowingly captive to other than the truth of God's gospel. I have been glad to number my days on earth by the passing seasons of the Calendar until time for me shall be no more. I pray that as we all learn better to number our days, applying our hearts to wisdom year after year, God will grant that "we may so pass through things temporal, that we finally lose not the things eternal."

Some More Reading

For evangelicals there is not a great deal of literature about the Church Year and its uses. There are understandable reasons for this since the Free Churches have not made the Calendar their own quite yet. Fortunately, the interest of evangelical Protestants in this area is growing; and the amount of writing on the subject may be expected to grow. Some of the older books mentioned here are out of print now but will well reward your search of old preachers' libraries or secondhand bookstores.

For a concise, practical outline of the Calendar nothing I know is better than the little pamphlet *The Christian Year*, first published by the Committee on Worship of the Federal Council of the Churches of Christ in America in 1937, and subsequently revised by Fred Winslow Adams, a Methodist, in 1940. Leaflet additions in the form of Calendars were published partially covering 1940 and for all of 1941, and later for 1948 through 1953. Adams acknowledges his considerable use of publications by the Commission on Evangelism and Devotional Life of the Congregational and Christian Churches, one by Raymond

Calkins entitled *The Christian Year,* published in 1936 as a leaflet, and one by Frederick I. Fagley, *A Guide for the Christian Year,* published in 1937 as a slightly longer pamphlet. Both were noteworthy antecedents to Adams's booklet, and I have been grateful to all three little publications for their introductory values as I began a serious study and use of the Calendar. Fortunate is the minister who can find copies of them today. They are well worth a search.

Here I wish to refer my readers to *Christian Worship* by George Hedley, published by Macmillan in 1953. Hedley, a Methodist, has written the most comprehensive and intelligible work I know about liturgical matters as they stand now in evangelical acceptance. Readers may wish to refer also to a compendium by Charles L. Wallis, *Worship Resources for the Christian Year.* Abingdon published in 1957 *Pastoral Prayers for the Church Year* by Samuel J. Schmiechen, an Evangelical and Reformed Church pastor. Evangelical and Reformed churchmen, while solidly Protestant, have good liturgical conditioning.

To our Anglican, Protestant Episcopalian, and Lutheran friends we must still look appreciatively for most of the writing about the Church Year. At the same time, it will be clear to evangelicals that much of what these friends have written has a liturgical orientation not yet fully shared by evangelical church people and even in some respects not likely ever to be accepted in Free Church life.

A classic in this category is Vernon Staley's *The Seasons, Fasts, and Festivals of the Christian Year.* This was published in 1910 by Mowbray & Co. of London and Oxford and has a distinctly Anglo-Catholic coloration, but it is a very comprehensive work albeit only 264 pages in length. It is based on the "Kalendar" of the Church of England. Much of it will have little homiletical value for American evangelicals, but it is important to know what is in this book if one is to have a general working knowledge of the Church Year.

A complementary work has been published as recently as 1957 by Edward T. Horn, III, an American Lutheran, through the Muhlenberg Press of Philadelphia. It is entitled *Christian Year.* It is technical and scholarly. Horn once served as a member of the Joint Commission on the Common Liturgy which represented a number of Lutheran bodies in America, and he previously participated in producing the Common Service Book, adopted by the United Lutheran Church in America. Methodists, Presbyterians, and such others will find his book informative and authoritative, and they may be helped especially by the scripture references listed for Calendar occasions both for use in preaching and for use as lessons. Like Provost Staley's book, however, Horn's is highly liturgical in both color and content. A liturgical manual, mainly for Disciples of Christ use, is *Christian Worship* by Edwin G. Osborn, which deserves the attention of Protestants generally.

On the other hand, George M. Gibson, a pastor of united Congregationalists and Presbyterians (writing, of course, as a Free Churchman), has produced *The Story of the Christian Year,* published by Abingdon Press in 1945. This book is written in a popular style, is not very technical, and is illustrated with numerous drawings from the related field of Christian symbolism. It is mainly historical, and it is not directly related to preaching or worship. It does, however, treat some of the American observances which Protestants in this country have added to their worship sequence, and one of its principal values is that it helps readers to apprehend the whole development from early Jewish to late American customs.

I can cite two other books of a similar nature. The first is *The Christian Year in Human Story* by Jane T. Stoddard, published without date by Hodder and Stoughton of London and probably out of print by now though possibly still in some circulation. The writer appears to be an Anglican, but in her preface she offers her collection of worship materials organized according to the Calendar with these words, "Now that the Church Festivals are so largely observed among Nonconformists in England, and also by Presbyterians in Scotland, while united services are becoming general throughout the country, I venture to hope that this book may be of interest to Christians of every name." I believe her hopes were justified. There is historical and devotional material in abundance, though not sermonic content as such. A more narrowly defined work of the same general kind is *The Story of Christmas* by R. J. Campbell of Chichester Cathedral, published in 1937 by the Macmillan Company in New York.

Books which deal with preaching and the Calendar are of two general categories, as I have come across them. There are books of sermons for Church Year seasons and occasions. Then there are books based on the Calendar which intend to provide texts, illustrations, and notes for sermons for some or all of the seasons and occasions.

In the last century the famous John Keble produced *Sermons for the Christian Year*. The only one of these books I have is Volume IV published in 1875-80 by Walter Smith of London. It contains sermons for Lent but none for Easter Sunday. I assume that there were prior volumes for other seasons, but an "Advertisement" in the front of my book leaves some question whether Keble lived long enough to complete volumes for Eastertide and "after Trinity." The modern preacher who wants to see how a great master set standards for Lenten preaching should hunt for this book, for of all the Church Year the Lenten season ought to challenge any preacher to be at his best in his pulpit.

British Methodism's Epworth Press in London has published three volumes of sermons by J. Ernest Rattenbury, which follow the Church Year. They are: *Adoration of the Lamb, O'er Every Foe Victorious*, and *The Throne, the Cradle, and the Star*. Here is evangelical preaching organized for the Calendar which makes the best possible use of both liturgical occasions and gospel witnessing. These little books will stimulate and energize a preacher to his best output.

H. Hughes Wagner, a Methodist minister, wrote *The Word in Season* published by Abingdon in 1951. This excellent title embraces sermons for each of the Calendar seasons. A short paragraph introduces the sermons for each season by setting forth in a sentence or two the significance of each season. His sermons are very good patterns.

A bridge between the two categories of books about Calendar preaching is *Preaching on Church and Community Occasions* by Ozora S. Davis, published in 1928 by the University of Chicago Press. To the Calendar occasions are added numerous other observances, such as national holidays and the like, and there seems to be more attention given to these than to strictly Church Year preaching. This probably reflects the actual attitude of evangelical Protestantism in 1928. However, the material for Advent, Lent, Pentecost Sunday, and Trinity Sunday is good. There are sermons as well as sermon notes for the occasions treated.

In 1939 Harper & Brothers of New York published *Preaching the Gospel* by Howard Chandler Robbins, an Episcopalian. However, it made considerable impression upon evangelicals at the time and is a collection of sermons of continuing worth.

Mention should also be made of *Preaching Theology* by Eric Baker, which Epworth Press published in London in 1954. More than sermon notes, yet not full length sermons, some of the chapters deal with the central gospel meanings of such Calendar observances as Advent, Palm Sunday, the Ascension, and Eastertide.

The second general category of books about preaching within the frame of the Church Year includes one by Paul B. Bull, published in 1938 by Macmillan, called *A Preacher's Note-Book*. The author is trying to teach young parsons how to prepare sermons and how to develop sermon materials, but since he is an avowed Anglo-Catholic, he just assumes that preaching naturally will follow the Calendar. Any preacher will find that this book contains considerable help for observing the Calendar in the pulpit, though an evangelical will not agree with Bull's general point of view.

Abingdon has just published in 1957 Paul E. Holdcraft's paperbound booklet *Texts and Themes for the Christian Year*, and Westminster Press of Philadelphia has published at the same time David A. MacLennan's longer book

Resources for Sermon Preparation. Both are gold mines for preachers, and both will be tempting to Saturday-night miners. Both are collections of Church Year materials. Holdcraft simply lists titles and texts; MacLennan develops texts and themes in slightly fuller degree.

Back in 1932 William H. Leach, a *Church Management* editor, and J. W. G. Ward, then minister of First Presbyterian Church in Oak Park, Illinois, collaborated in producing for the Cokesbury Press of Nashville *The Tragedy and Triumph of Easter.* This book includes not only sermonic suggestions but orders of worship and devotions for Lent as well as Easter. In those days many evangelicals were not using the word "Lent" itself in titles.

Charles L. Wallis has compiled *Worship Resources for the Christian Year* and *Speakers' Illustrations for Special Days.* Harpers published the first in 1954, and Abingdon, the second in 1956. They are mentioned here only because of their use of the Calendar as a basis for arrangement.

Once again evangelicals may be indebted, gladly, to Episcopalians for what is probably the most serious book on the Calendar published in the 1950's. It is a compendium edited by Howard A. Johnson entitled *Preaching the Christian Year,* published in New York by Charles Scribner's Sons in 1957. It is not, however, a collection of sermons. It only intends to offer treatments by a number of well-known writers of the basic theology for each main season or occasion of the Church Year. But this is so well done and is so well arranged in terms of the Calendar that it surely will mean a very great deal to preachers.

While the books mentioned by no means exhaust the number on the subject of the Church Year, they do represent an attempt to provide fellow evangelicals with a working knowledge of the Calendar itself and of sources from which preaching guidance is available, guidance which evangelicals can use at any stage of liturgical development within the Free Churches of America. For these purposes more than a formal listing of a bibliography has been offered here. Let us hope that the rapid pace with which new books in this field are now appearing will gain even more momentum. Evangelical Protestantism needs its own extensive literature in this area.

Index of Bible Passages

Index of Persons and Subjects